Regulation, Economics, and the Law

Regulation, Economics, and the Law

Edited by
Bernard H. Siegan
University of San Diego School of Law

LexingtonBooks
D.C. Heath and Company
Lexington, Massachusetts
Toronto

Library of Congress Cataloging in Publication Data

Main entry under title:
  Regulation, economics, and the Law.

  Consists mainly of revisions of 6 debates hosted by the University of San Diego Law School in the winter of 1977.
  1. Trade regulation—United States—Addresses, essays, lectures. 2. Industry and state—United States—Addresses, essays, lectures. 3. Liberty of speech—United States—Addresses, essays, lectures. I. Siegan, Bernard H.
KF1600.A75R4   343'.73'07   77-11398
ISBN 0-669-02091-5

Published simultaneously in Canada

Printed in the United States of America

International Standard Book Number: 0-669-02901-5

Library of Congress Catalog Card Number: 77-11398

Contents

Preface

In the winter of 1977, the University of San Diego Law School hosted six debates on current economic and social issues. Each of these debates together with a summary of rebuttals and answers to questions from the audience constitutes a chapter in this book. The original presentations and subsequent comments were recorded and transcribed, and the speakers were given an opportunity to revise their remarks for publication. The series, which was open to the public, was part of my course, "Law and Economics."

Five of the debates revolve about a theme common to much public discussion of our time—the necessity and desirability of government regulation. The core issues were the same in all these debates: Will the private market better provide for the wants, desires, needs, and aspirations of the people in the presence of or in the absence of regulation? Which model serves us more efficiently and effectively? Will governmental supervision of private activity allocate resources more efficiently and equitably? The debate on corporate social responsibility concerned these issues only tangentially. The underlying question of this topic was the extent to which the profit motive serves the community.

The book's final chapter is based on a speech given by Professor Milton Friedman at the dedication of the law school's Joseph P. Grace courtroom on November 7, 1977. It is relevant to the subject matter of the debates because in his speech Professor Friedman compared public response to and acceptance of restrictions placed on the exercise of First Amendment rights and those placed on the exercise of economic rights.

Our distinguished debaters responded well to their challenges, not only augmenting our knowledge of the subject matter with which they dealt but also stimulating our thinking about other economic and social controversies relevant to our time.

The debate series furthered the audience's knowledge about current events. It did not, however, relate directly to issues of law, or the operation of our legal system. Understandably, some may question the value of such a series for students training for a career in the law. Economists may wonder whether the tradeoff between the time devoted to such a series and the time that would otherwise be spent in traditional legal education is advantageous to the students. I feel it is, because I do not believe that a line exists clearly demarking the concerns of the law. Future lawyers, judges, and legislators will be better prepared to serve their professional interests by having greater familiarity with and understanding of contemporary approaches to solving society's economic and social problems.

Perhaps it would be comforting to believe that legal controversies can be solved by reference to an existing body of law containing an array of precedents awaiting application. However, precedents are not always readily available, and their applicability is a matter of considerable discretion. Entering into that discretion to a substantial degree are the policy-making propensities of judges. Referring to the manner in which a judge selects among the interests constantly competing for his approval, Justice Benjamin Cardozo once candidly described the process as follows:

> If you ask how he [a judge] is to know when one interest outweighs another, I can only answer that he must get his knowledge just as the legislator gets it, from experience and study and reflection; in brief, from life itself. Here indeed, is the point of contact between the legislator's work and his. The choice of methods, the appraisement of values, must in the end be guided by like considerations for the one as for the other. Each indeed is legislating within the limits of his competence.[1]

Accordingly, the give and take among authorities on current topics should prove valuable to both future lawyers and judges who may one day confront similar or comparable issues. In particular, the debates in this volume should help provide an understanding of the operation of the market and of government regulation and eliminate at least some conjecture about the final impact of a decision affecting the marketplace.

Experience of our judicial system reveals that opinions are quite often result-oriented. Legal commentators frequently are able to explain major court decisions in light more of social and economic preferences of the justices than of existing precedents. Significant periods of judicial history are marked by the predisposition of a high court toward particular schools of economic thinking. For many, this may not be the "proper" or "preferred" way, but it is the reality—a fact that training in the law must recognize.

Note

1. Benjamin N. Cardozo, *The Nature of the Judicial Process* (New Haven: Yale University Press, 1921), p. 113.

Regulation, Economics, and the Law

1

Should There Be Greater Government Regulation of Our Energy Future?

Stewart L. Udall and
M. Bruce Johnson

Stewart L. Udall

For three years I have been warning that in all likelihood the next critical development in energy would be natural gas shortages, and today we are experiencing the truth of that prediction. Now that I have established some degree of credibility as a prophet, I will venture another prediction: If President Carter does not address the problem directly, and if the country does not cooperate in reaching an alternative solution, the next shock our nation will suffer will be gasoline rationing and the rationing of all liquid fuels. In his February 8, 1977, press conference President Carter said that during the previous two months the United States had imported 50 percent of its crude oil. Our oil bill in 1973 was $7 billion; in 1976 it was $35 billion. If such increases continue, we will soon be in a situation in which we simply cannot afford to import more oil. Rationing therefore will be forced upon us by default.

My answer to the question of whether in the near future the government should more strictly regulate energy production is "Yes." I fear that our political process makes such action inevitable. However, I am not in favor of regulation simply for regulation's sake. I do concede that had we followed different policies in the past, we might not be in our current predicament and thus might not have the need to regulate energy production. Nevertheless, we must accept the fact that we are facing a serious and prolonged problem. Because no easy solutions to this problem are now apparent, I feel that we have no choice but to continue temporary price controls. The emergency bill that the president submitted to Congress in March 1977 that attempts to deal with the current natural gas shortages confers even greater regulatory powers in government agencies than those they now have.

Moreover, the contest between producer and consumer states is just beginning. Last year Wyoming and Montana enacted legislation levying high severance taxes on coal and uranium. Thus even the states are responding to the present crisis by regulating energy production through higher taxes and stricter environmental safeguards. Why must we have more such regulation? The answer is simple—because our country is in the grip of severe energy shortages that make easy solutions impossible.

I suspect that our main disagreement in this forum centers not only on our

1

basic assumptions but also on our assessment of the facts. I am convinced that
our national assumptions concerning energy have long been incorrect. We have
misconceived the causes of our current predicament. In my opinion no production solution is possible, for we have recklessly allowed these shortages to
develop in our country. The source of this reckless attitude can be found in the
spectacular post-World War II economic growth that gave United States citizens
the purchasing power that they had coveted during the long period of lean living
and Spartan sacrifices that had spanned the years between the onset of the
Depression and the end of the war. The American oil industry had performed
excellently for the Allies, and in 1945 its leaders were in an uncommonly
bullish frame of mind. They had placed the United States in the position of
producing and using well over half the world's oil, and they had secured that
position by discovering and leasing giant oil fields in the Middle East and South
America.

This was an intoxicating time for the industry. True, an oil glut existed,
and production therefore had to be temporarily decreased, but this fact posed
small difficulties. In addition almost everyone believed that enough oil could
be found to fill the country's needs far into the twenty-first century. Such
optimism seemed, at that time, to be justified. Drilling was at a very high level
during the immediate postwar period, and our proven reserves increased every
year until 1961.

But the energy roller coaster picked up momentum in the 1960s. The oil
industry considered that a production glut was the big problem, and a nation-
wide campaign was launched to encourage travel and increase all petroleum
uses. These efforts succeeded far beyond the industry's expectations. Overall
growth continued at a 5 percent annual rate, and an oil import quota imposed
by the government in 1958 protected the greater part of the American market
for domestic producers.

During these halcyon days of growing consumption, no national energy
policy was in force. Or, to be more precise, the policy was laissez faire; the oil
companies were allowed to decide which course to follow. Energy policy issues
were purposely kept out of the political arena. This result was possible for
several reasons, but perhaps the most important was that the public was content
with the low prices charged for gasoline and natural gas. Additionally the oil
industry had great influence in the major political parties. Ironically, the government's own petroleum experts in fact misled everyone by publishing "official"
estimates of our potential petroleum reserves that were even more optimistic
than those of the oil industry.

However, by the early 1970s several warning signals appeared to mar the
sky-is-the-limit expectations of both the industry and the public. United States
oil production peaked and started to decline in November 1970; the widening
gap between U.S. production and consumption required substantial annual

increases in foreign imports to prevent crippling shortages; and, most alarming of all, world oil consumption reached such a high level that a seller's market developed. The result was that the inept OPEC [Organization of Petroleum Exporting Countries] organization was suddenly in the driver's seat. Clearly, the United States had grossly misjudged its petroleum reserves and was trying to formulate an ad hoc energy policy without any real agreement on how much oil was left.

Thus we find ourselves on the threshold of a major energy crisis that will cripple our economy unless programs of retrenchment and conservation are initiated and carried out. Oil and natural gas continue to provide approximately 75 percent of the energy Americans now consume. In order to understand the natural gas crisis in the United States, one only need look at the energy we expend on transportation. Today, for example, American users are burning more than half the gasoline in the world. And half the remaining petroleum being used in the United States today comes from natural gas. Moreover, during the last three years the experts on the Federal Power Commission have been warning that our reserves of natural gas are declining rapidly. The trend is unmistakable: We are running out of petroleum. This is the reality that has produced a national debate over energy controls.

Official figures reveal that in all probability we have already exhausted over half our oil and natural gas supplies, that our known reserves constitute another quarter, and that another quarter is yet to be discovered. The statistics also tell us that we have found all the "easy" oil and that most of that which remains lies either on the continental shelf, in small pools onshore, or in much deeper strata in the earth. It is inescapable that tomorrow's oil will be costlier than today's.

This is the situation in which we have placed ourselves by squandering these irreplaceable resources. When a nation acts recklessly and thus creates severe shortages of a vital commodity, its choices are limited: It can resort to rationing—a step that we have not yet had to take but one to which we are perilously close—or it can institute some kind of controls in an attempt to assure that the shortages will be shared equitably.

I am increasingly of the opinion that the period in which we are living will someday be known as the Petroleum Age. Our modern system of energy production brings power to people in an instant. Flip a switch and there is light. Turn a dial and there is heat or cool air or a bevy of energy-slaves to do our bidding. Press the ignition and time and space are left quickly behind. However, the Petroleum Age has entered its decline, and no meaningful substitutes for our rapidly diminishing oil reserves are in sight. In economic terms a viable substitute has to be available both in the same quantity and at approximately the same cost as the original resource. Thus if a person opened a San Diego service station selling a substitute for gasoline that cost $55 a gallon, this development would not be much of a solution to our energy crisis. This dilemma, stated starkly, is the energy crisis. It is a major occurrence—one that will change the course of our history and dominate our lives for several decades.

Moreover, we are now confronted with having to admit that we have made spectacular miscalculations about the power of technology to crank up quick-fix solutions.

We Americans emerged from World War II infatuated with scientific miracles and firmly believing that the same minds that had unlocked the secrets of the atom could solve any other physical problem. Above all, we believed— and our most prominent thinkers repeatedly asserted—that the atomic age had answered the question of where the world would find its future energy supplies.

A short generation later, even after the Arab oil embargo had revealed our dependence on imported oil, we clung to the myth of the technological solution. It was Project Independence, which, "in the spirit of Apollo, with the determination of the Manhattan Project," pledged that our scientists would develop the means to make the United States self-sufficient in energy by 1980.

From today's sober perspective, it is difficult to recall our technological optimism in its prime. Nevertheless, Americans at midcentury universally and eagerly accepted the idea of unlimited resources, of "free" atomic energy that would eliminate any resource shortages. The idea was accepted partly because our history has largely been one of the increasingly successful exploitation of resources through technological innovation.

Since the onset of World War II, when our technological revolution began, we have continually deluded ourselves that we are so inventive that we can create miracle substitutes for any resource. An overwhelming number of American people seem to assume that science can solve the energy problem. I now believe that many of the so-called technological miracles of recent years have their source in cheap petroleum. Some contemporary technologists act as though machines run on their own power source. However, although we have always known that all machines require energy, we are just now learning how important that energy is. Recent events tell us that some business and energy executives made enormous misjudgments about natural gas supplies. For example, despite the warnings of the Federal Power Commission, substitute energy sources were not developed. Big oil interests, who clung to the old myths that had served them well in the past, continued to prate that if we let them make huge profits, they would find more petroleum and eliminate the shortages that are plaguing us.

Any country will flounder if its leaders base vital national policies on misjudgments and illusions. It is increasingly clear that we cannot master our energy crisis so long as our policy making ignores hard truths. In 1973, for example, we were planning extravagant consumption for the future and operating on the erroneous assumption that we are still the world's petroleum powerhouse when, in fact, we were slowly becoming an oil have-not nation.

Likewise, our Washington planners were pretending that we would soon discover vast oil reserves on our continental shelves that would keep the pipelines flowing when, in fact, important questions about how much offshore oil exists remain unanswered. Many economists, who nurture their own set of illusions, were acting as though much higher prices for crude oil would create a kind of magic suction pump that would overnight increase the output of American oil wells and thus bring supply and demand into balance.

Our predicament will continue to worsen so long as we continue to base our policies on such self-deception. An historic blunder has occurred. We are making an oil policy without first deciding how much oil we have left. We are asking our oil industry to make big increases in production without knowing whether it can do so. Thus when the consumption of natural gas, America's biggest growth industry, quadrupled between 1950 and 1970, we set the stage for shortages by assuming that gas production would continue to increase indefinitely.

This technological optimism has betrayed us; during the past four years our oil and natural gas production has been declining steadily at rates of 5 to 8 percent a year. Unfortunately the free market is capable of doing little to increase production when an irreplaceable resource is vanishing. The price of oil could be raised $25 tomorrow; the price of natural gas trebled or quadrupled, and I grant you that very modest increases in production might occur. However, no matter how high prices rise, production cannot be increased enough to cope with the serious shortages that lie ahead. Petroleum is a nonrenewable resource; only a finite amount of it exists. Thus if we decide to pump it all out as soon as possible and consume it at a faster rate, we will succeed in running out in fourteen or fifteen years instead of sixteen or twenty.

The fact of the matter is that a democratic country that overreaches its energy resources must have a national policy to deal with the shortages that ensue. Unfortunately we have never developed such a policy for energy, for so long as petroleum was cheap and seemed to be inexhaustible, we nurtured the illusion that shortages would not occur. In addition we have not had a national energy policy because with three-fourths of our energy coming from petroleum, the oil companies did not want one. OPEC, the international cartel, is now calling the shots, and OPEC wants nothing to do with the laws of the free market. Until very recently oil was not only our least-regulated industry but also the one enjoying the most favorable tax treatment. The oil depletion allowance, the most generous tax law on the books, created a policy that in effect said, "It is in the national interest to discover and consume our oil as fast as possible." Until three or four years ago this approach was our real national energy policy, and almost everyone assumed that it would continue.

As a result of this "policy," and because we are at this moment confronted with shortages, the nation's options are limited. Moreover, the perspective in which each of the proposed long-term alternatives is evaluated is crucial.

Under the "cheap energy" policy of the past, nearly all the major decisions were made by energy companies that were influenced by the pulling and hauling of marketplace economics, by government policies that promoted the production of cheap energy, and by the companies' own selfish desire to increase sales of the fuel that they were producing. These industries continue to control the production and distribution of energy in this country. Thus, if the various options are to be seriously considered, all conflicting values must be weighed so that balanced policies can eventually be formulated.

One such choice (embodied in our present set of controls and regulations) is to allocate the shortages in such a way that we treat different regions the same way economically and protect our overall economy as best we can. We are now importing over 40 percent of our oil, and most of that goes to the eastern seaboard. What should we do? Should we force the eastern states to pay OPEC prices and allow the rest of the country to pay the domestic price? Or should we equalize prices and thus share the burden of shortages until we can reestablish a free market situation?

A second option in combating shortages is, of course, conservation. In fact during the next few years, this approach will be imperative. Thus the primary task now is to develop a frugal national life-style that conserves and husbands oil supplies in order to prolong the Petroleum Age as far as possible. This generation will be anathema to its children and grandchildren if it plunders its continental shelves, or overpumps its existing wells, on the assumption that the present is responsible only for the present, while the future is the future's problem. President Carter himself has been making this point, and I rather like the low-profile manner with which he has handled this issue. He seems to believe that the energy crisis is a complex, long-term problem and that we must work together and make sacrifices if we are to ameliorate the situation.

Another option—albeit a dangerous one—is available. We can continue to import more oil. Richard Nixon said that we would be independent of imports by 1980. Yet 1980 is almost here, and we are becoming more dependent each month. With regard to natural gas one option is to develop a number of extremely costly LNG [liquefied natural gas] tankers and to import Algerian, Libyan, or Indonesian gas that will cost four or five times as much as domestic gas. But how far down that road of increasing dependence do we want to go?

A fourth option is to eliminate shortages by producing alternate forms of energy. But what were the schemes that we bragged about in 1974? Two of the supposed answers to OPEC were coal gasification and production of oil from shale. However, as yet not a single coal gasification or oil shale plant is operating in the United States. The technology remains unproven, and today the economics of these schemes is uncertain. All the alternatives face enormous problems. Expectations of a future mixed-energy society must be tempered by the realization that significantly altering the vast, complex energy systems that now exist will take fifteen to twenty years; for in addition to the strictly technological questions, formidable interrelated economic, environmental, and social obstacles must be overcome.

The perplexing irony of the alternate-energy transition is that nearly every alternative will require substantial oil to replace oil, making the development of some alternative sources that much more difficult and expensive. Whether one considers the fuel necessary for mining and refining, or the fuel for transportation and distribution of the new sources, some petroleum will be necessary for developing alternate energy sources.

As I stated earlier, I am convinced that eliminating all government controls will not bring about any substantial increase in production in the near future. For example, 1974, the year after the embargo, was the best year that the oil companies have ever had. They showed record profits, and they almost doubled the amount of new drilling over the 1973 figure. Nevertheless, they found only eight trillion cubic feet of new natural gas reserves in that year of record exploration, at the same time we were using nearly twenty trillion. Because our natural gas reserves have diminished sharply during the last few years, our options are narrowing, and conservation appears as the only rational alternative in the immediate future.

One additional argument can be made for price controls. The electric power companies, for example, are regulated monopolies. Yet one does not hear people saying, "Let's remove the controls and allow the companies to charge whatever they want, for they will then produce more." Because the industry is regulated, it is assured a fair return on its investments. Regulation is part of the game, and with electric power it has been from the beginning. The natural gas industry is another partially regulated industry that is also a monopoly. We must not forget that when a pipeline enters a home, it is the only source of energy the residents of that house have.

I have no quarrel with the theory of free market economics; I regret that Congress regulated natural gas prices at the wellhead and wish that President Nixon had not, in 1971, imposed the price controls on petroleum that were continued when all other price controls were phased out a few years ago.

Economists have now announced (with oil industry executives loudly chorusing their support) that the best way to resolve our energy problem is to throw off all controls and let the imperatives of the marketplace sort things out. Yet, on closer examination this elegantly simple solution turns out to be a political nettle that recent presidents and Congresses have been unable to grasp. Why is this so? Why has the energy issue been so intractable, so seemingly immune to straightforward economic solutions?

The answer is that once political considerations permeate any economic issue, simple, straightforward solutions are rarely acceptable when economic decisions that affect everyone must be made. It sounds rational to say, "Let's go back to the free market." However, when any plan for a return to an uncontrolled market involves billion-dollar increases in the value of existing oil and gas reserves combined with corresponding billion-dollar increases in the prices that consumers must pay for these same resources, any legislative body attuned to the opinions of those who vote—that is, the same consumers described above—will vote against any short-term scheme for decontrol.

The hitch is that consumer-minded congressmen cannot defend the massive transfer of wealth from consumers to producers that would be involved in rapid decontrol. This is the reason that Congress is sharply divided on the decontrol issue: Representatives from producer states favor it, and consumer representatives are unalterably opposed. It is that simple.

In any event I submit that it is misleading to argue that if the government allows the "natural forces of the free market" full sway, price increases would soon eliminate energy shortages. Unfortunately, this dogma, dear to the hearts of economists and oil interests, raises at least one question for each answer it provides. When a nation is firmly in the grip of a cartel, is it not too late for the price mechanism alone to ride to the rescue? Does it make sense to talk glibly about supply and demand producing "substitutes" for oil when the only substitutes in sight will cost three or four times as much and fill only a fraction of the nation's needs? And, politically speaking, when absolute shortages loom, is it acceptable to pursue an economic theory that translates into the commandment: "Every person for himself, and let the weak fend for themselves?"

These considerations mean that the only possible political compromise is gradual decontrol through a series of steps that are reasonably equitable to all parties.

As a conservationist, arguing for further controls pains me, for I know full well that low prices encourage users of energy to waste precious petroleum supplies. However, the political realities, not wrongheaded economic thinking, prevent a rapid return to the competitive pricing of petroleum. All economic issues ultimately dissolve into politics. This is the overriding reality in any democracy!

M. Bruce Johnson

In recent weeks the natural gas shortage in the eastern United States has caused the layoff of perhaps as many as two million factory workers. Office buildings have been closed. The governor of Pennsylvania shut down both public and private schools. Some states have been declared disaster areas. Widespread economic and physical hardships have been experienced by the citizens of the affected areas.

Surely it is appropriate to inquire why the natural gas crisis occurred. What are the causes of the latest "energy gap"?

Some politicians suggest that nature is at fault for giving us an extraordinarily cold winter. The governor of Ohio urged his fellow citizens to pray for warmth. Our new president demonstrated moral leadership, according to the media, by turning White House thermostats down to sixty-five degrees even though this caused the air conditioning units to go on. The governor of New Jersey ordered the residents of his state to set their thermostats down to sixty-five degrees on threat of fines and jail sentences.

But few of the politicians chose to admit that their own regulations—their price and allocation controls—are the cause of the shortage or energy gap. Instead of admitting that price controls discouraged production and encouraged consumption, the politicians opted for prayer, moral leadership, and threats of jail sentences. I suggest that an energy policy which leads to the imprisonment of people for adjusting the temperature of their homes to suit their own health needs and comfort levels is regulation that has failed. Is crime in the furnace room to take the place of crime in the streets as our government's main concern?

I argue that there should be less government regulation of our energy future; I base my case on the record of past government regulation in the energy sector. The natural gas shortage is topical and so I direct most of my attention to that sector. If time permitted, a similar chronicle of shortsighted regulatory and statutory mismanagement could be developed for all energy areas. Natural gas, oil, coal, and nuclear energy have been consciously or inadvertently mismanaged by our government agencies. I will highlight some of these errors and will then turn to the subject of conservation—the latest so-called solution advanced by the politicians.

Let's take a quick look at the effects of regulation of natural gas in the United States. In 1938 Congress passed the Natural Gas Act which placed pipelines selling gas in interstate commerce under the control of the Federal Power Commission. At the time, the act specifically exempted the production and collection of natural gas and so the price of natural gas at the wellhead was not subject to regulation. In 1954 the Supreme Court ruled in the *Phillips Petroleum Company* v. *Wisconsin* case that gas sold in interstate commerce was subject to regulation by the Federal Power Commission. And so price regulation began.

The number of domestic oil and gas wells drilled had been rising steadily following the removal of price controls at the end of World War II. After natural gas price controls were imposed in 1954–55, the number of wells drilled per year peaked. As it became less and less economically feasible to engage in drilling activities a steady decline began, lasting into the 1970s. When some price increases were permitted in 1973, there was an immediate boost in drilling activity once again. The regulated price of 52¢ per thousand cubic feet obviously reduced the incentive to produce additional gas. However, since gas sold intrastate was exempt from regulation, drillers concentrated their activities in states where the gas could be sold at competitive prices. Hence, intrastate gas sells for approximately $2 while interstate gas from wells started since 1974 sells at the price of $1.44, set by the Federal Power Commission recently. Gas discovered before 1973 is pegged at 29.5¢. Because of these multitiered price controls and because of the existence of long-term contracts signed at earlier lower prices, the average of all gas flowing through interstate pipelines is approximately 56¢ per thousand cubic feet.

Natural gas price controls assure the consumer that he will not have to pay the unregulated price of $2; they also assure him that he won't get the gas. Hence, controls led to the recent crisis and to President Carter's decision to let interstate buyers bid for the interstate gas at "fair" market prices. Beyond the current crisis, the choice politicians face is whether to continue price controls and shortages or whether to deregulate and allow the gas to flow unimpeded to its highest-valued uses. Immediate deregulation of natural gas will not instantly solve the problems that have been over twenty years in the making by the politicians and their controls. But deregulation would have the effect of encouraging conservation of natural gas as consumers face higher prices. It would also have the effect of encouraging drillers to assume the risk of going after the less accessible, more expensive natural gas. And, it would encourage owners of natural gas to tap and deliver existing proven sources.

The politicians and the media accuse some of the natural gas owners of "withholding" natural gas supplies in anticipation of higher prices. This is playing politics with a vengeance. It is always convenient to find a scapegoat on whom to blame the results of your own mismanagement. Thus, the politicians insinuate that anyone who withholds natural gas at regulated prices is unpatriotic, un-American, greedy, and profiteering.

I have no good data on the amount and extent of hoards of natural gas nor, do I believe, does anyone else. However, I would not be surprised if such hoards did exist. Why should the owner of natural gas voluntarily make a gift or subsidy of $1.50 per thousand cubic feet to gas users whose congressmen have been responsible for the current legislation? If gas is worth $2 in the free intrastate market, why put it in the hands of people who value it only at 50¢? Why contribute to waste?

If the government fixed the price of oranges in interstate commerce at 50¢ a dozen, would we blame the orange producer if he sold his oranges in-state at an unregulated price of $2 a dozen? If the increased value of the inventory (whether it be natural gas or oranges) is thought to be unearned and therefore immoral, why haven't the politicians called for price controls on single-family dwellings in southern California? Various local governments have deliberately adopted no-growth land use policies that have increased the price of existing homes at a rate far beyond the general rate of inflation. The unearned capital gains that homeowners have received or will receive are no more justified or moral than the windfalls that owners of natural gas or crude oil would receive at market prices. If the government can freeze the price of natural gas and crude oil, what in principle prevents it from controlling the sales prices of homes?

The answer, of course, is that there is no difference in principle. Rather, it is a matter of politics. Philosophical and legal issues aside, the owners of single-family dwellings are politically more potent than the owners of natural gas or crude oil supplies. The long tradition of private property rights in common law notwithstanding, if the politicians decide in their usual ad hoc, pragmatic fashion that it is politically in their interest to expropriate a particular subset of the population, they will. And if they can do it to the Exxon Corporation, the nation's biggest gas producer and one of the largest industrial corporations, they can do it to each one of us when our turn comes.

Now let's turn to petroleum price and allocation controls. The petroleum industry in the United States is the most completely and elaborately controlled industry in the country and perhaps even in the world. Beginning with general wage and price controls established in August 1971, the United States government has controlled the prices of domestic crude oil and petroleum products. When the Cost of Living Council and the Economic Stabilization Act expired on April 30, 1974, government control of the petroleum industry continued under the Emergency Petroleum Allocation Act of 1973. As each new set of controls led to problems and complications, additional legislation was adopted to meet the new problems—in particular, the Energy Policy and Conservation Act of December 22, 1975 (sometimes called the Cold Homes and Closed Factories Act).

In general, we can summarize four elements of the controls: First, there is Federal Energy Administration control of the price of crude oil produced in the United States. Second, there is FEA control over prices of products which are made out of crude oil. Third, there is FEA control over the allocation of crude oil and products produced in the United States—who must offer to sell to whom and on what terms. And fourth, there is the entitlements program.

Why did the government develop a regulation and control program that virtually amounts to running the petroleum business on a day-to-day basis? The answer begins with the OPEC cartel. From 1950 to 1973, competition among oil companies had forced the real price of oil steadily downward. Then the OPEC cartel formed in 1973. The members of OPEC have sufficient petroleum reserves to enable them to set the international price of crude oil by manipulating the rate of output of crude from OPEC fields. Since the amount of crude oil demanded on the world market is not very responsive in the short run to increases in the price of crude, OPEC can restrict supplies, raise the world price, and increase its revenues. It is important to realize that the higher OPEC price does not reflect proportionally increased production costs. The marginal cost of the crude they sell at $12-$13 is 50¢. Nor are OPEC prices high because they are afraid of running out. For example, Iran can produce six million barrels daily (assuming 40 percent recovery) for forty-five years—and that assumes no new discoveries. The history of the petroleum industry is characterized by gluts of oil and corresponding downward pressures on prices. The OPEC cartel temporarily changed that by withholding output. All oil from whatever source now becomes valued at the OPEC-established price. The price is not entirely arbitrary since it is linked to the cost of developing alternative energy sources. The oil price is set just below the cost of the next best alternative fuel. If OPEC becomes too greedy, it will pay producers outside of the cartel to invest in facilities for exploration and for extraction of oil from shale and tar sands, for accelerated production of coal, geothermal, nuclear, solar, and other potential sources of power. Thus, there is an upper limit in practice to the price that OPEC can establish and maintain since we would expect users and other producers (if allowed) to shift to alternative sources of energy as OPEC's oil becomes more and more expensive.

The politicians tell us that we should reduce our dependence on imported oil by reducing our consumption and by increasing our domestic production of energy. However, consider what the government has done rather than what it has said. First, by its control of domestic crude and refined product prices at lower-than-equilibrium levels, the government encourages consumption at these arbitrarily low prices. We will use more oil at $5 than at $13 a barrel. Although the delivered price of foreign oil is over $13 a barrel, the regulations force domestic owners of so-called old oil or lower-tier oil to sell at prices recently in the neighborhood of $5.18 per forty-two-gallon barrel. Newly discovered domestic oil is controlled at approximately $11.40 a barrel, but the "Mom and Pop" stripper well operators are permitted to sell at the high international price. One of the major features of the 1975 act was to roll back the price of domestic crude from an average of $8.75 per barrel to $7.66 effective February 1, 1976. With domestic crude prices fixed at these low levels and with the strict control of cost pass-throughs and markups, the price of refined petroleum products is subsidized. The lower price encourages the U.S. consumer to use more rather than less energy. Although the stated goal is energy conservation, the effect is redistribution—the petroleum price controls subsidize the heavy users of petroleum products at the expense of the lighter users and at the expense of the producers.

In addition to discouraging the wise use of energy, these policies also discourage the production of petroleum products. Admittedly the higher upper-tier price for new oil is supposed to finesse the economic disincentive effects of price controls. However, any producer with half a grain of sense knows that today's new oil can become, by the stroke of the congressional pen, tomorrow's old oil. Congress has frozen prices and rolled back prices before and can reasonably be expected to do it again. Hence, every oil producer must now crank the capricious political factors into his expectations when he contemplates explorations, drilling, or other long-term investments. The prudent manager of an energy company might today best serve his stockholders if he diversified away from the overregulated energy field.

Naturally, when prices of various categories of domestic crude were frozen at different levels, the impact was felt unevenly by various refiners. Some refiners purchased most of their crude on the international market at world prices. Others were heavily dependent on upper-tier domestic crude oil. Still others had long-term contracts or title to old domestic oil. Clearly, those refiners who had access to proportionately large amounts of the low-priced old domestic oil had an economic advantage over their competitors. Therefore, if Refiner A had access to $5.18 crude oil, he would be required to price his products at a low level because of the way the product price control rules work. Hence, the price of Refiner A's products would be considerably lower than the price of refined products produced and sold by Refiner B who might be purchasing his crude at the higher cartel price. With uncharacteristic insight (probably provided by Refiner B), the government recognized that this price differential would prompt consumers to favor the products of Refiner A at the expense of Refiner B. Refiner A and firms like him would grow at the expense of firms like Refiner B who were dependent on higher-cost foreign crude oil.

In order to prevent such changes in the relative fortunes of different refiners, the government developed what has been called the entitlements program. The purpose of this program is to patch over the cracks caused by the price control program. In principle, the entitlements program is supposed to equalize the cost of crude oil for each refiner. Those who have access to relatively large amounts of the old crude oil whose price is arbitrarily fixed at $5.18 must pay a premium in order to secure government authority to refine their own oil. The premium, in turn, is transferred to refiners which have higher-cost crude oil. The transfer of the dollar premium takes place in the form of purchasing an entitlement. Those refiners who have the high-cost oil are given entitlements by the government. Those refiners with low-cost oil must buy these entitlements. In principle, the costs of crude become roughly the same to each refiner. The FEA calculates the entitlement price and determines, on a monthly basis, how many entitlements each firm must buy or sell in order to conduct its refining operations.

It is commonly known that regulations beget regulations. The side effects and spillover effects of regulations create the incentive for still more controls and regulations. Hence, the two-tier price controls on oil led to the entitlements program which was supposed to give all refiners more equitable access to the lower-priced oil in order to prevent the change in market shares that would surely result from the two-tier pricing system. So, the government initially imposed regulations on oil prices and now finds itself imposing regulations to freeze the structure of the domestic refining industry to conform to the pattern that existed at an arbitrary date prior to the OPEC cartel. This has the effect of diminishing competition.

There is, of course, a special provision for small refiners. They receive additional entitlements on a sliding scale so that the smaller the refiner, the more additional entitlements he receives from the FEA. Small refiners have also been excused from purchasing entitlements for some or all of their crude oil.

Since smaller refiners are typically higher-cost refiners, the waste of resources involved in the subsidy is apparent. The entitlements program has shifted crude oil away from refiners with low marginal costs toward firms with high marginal costs. This results in a deadweight loss to consumers.

Yet, the greatest unanticipated effect of the entitlements program was to increase our dependence on foreign sources of crude oil. Consider the case of a refiner whose share of imported oil is greater than the industry's share as of that magic date established by the regulations. For each barrel of additional oil this refiner imports at the OPEC price of, say, $13.50, he receives a fraction of an entitlement from the FEA. This entitlement has an artificial market value created by the regulations. Thus, the net cost to the refiner of an additional barrel of OPEC oil is equal to the $13.50 minus the proceeds of the sale of his entitlement. Since the net price is less than the gross price, the refiner is encouraged to import more OPEC oil. Consequently, oil imports rise. In effect, the entitlements program subsidizes the importation of OPEC oil.

When you buy a gallon of gasoline refined from Arab crude oil you pay less than the full price, due to FEA regulations; when you buy a gallon of gasoline refined from domestic crude, you pay more than the American producer receives. The extra amount goes to the Arabs! In sum, you buy more gas because of FEA control, and you help maintain the high OPEC price.

This result is widely accepted by students of the energy sector. Indeed, in a December 1976 Federal Trade Commission staff report on the effects of federal price and allocation regulations on the petroleum industry, we find the following statement.

> The entitlements program, like the cost pass-through regulations for refined products, caused more crude oil to be imported than would have been the case in an unregulated market. Like the cost pass-through regulations, the entitlements program tended to cause the retail price of refined products to be lower than the true marginal social cost of producing them. The true cost to society of another barrel of crude oil input to the production of refined products was the world price ex tariff . . . because of the entitlements program, however, the refiner's marginal cost was lower . . . ; and it is the refiner's marginal cost that is reflected in the market price of products. Since consumers did not pay the marginal social cost for petroleum products, they tended to consume more than would have been dictated by efficient resource allocation. As with the cost pass-through regulations, the effect was to use rents extracted from producers of old crude oil to subsidize the production and consumption of petroleum products. Since imported crude oil was the marginal crude oil, increased imports supported the increased consumption. Economic efficiency would have been improved had less resources been devoted to purchasing foreign crude oil and had these resources been used, instead, to provide more non-petroleum products.[1]

How can the results be any clearer? In the course of muddling through by adding patchwork regulations here and there, the authorities have discouraged production, shifted crude oil to higher-cost refiners, encouraged consumption through lower prices, and stimulated the importation of foreign crude oil from the OPEC cartel members. Each of these results which can be directly traced to specific federal regulations is precisely the opposite of the stated goals of our so-called energy policy.

Perhaps we shouldn't be surprised since politicians frequently say one thing and do another. Yet, I believed them when they called for an energy policy that would encourage the domestic production of natural gas and crude oil; I believed them when they called for domestic conservation of energy; and I believed them when they urged less dependence on foreign sources of oil. And I am still convinced that these are or should be the goals of a national energy policy.

How can our goals be achieved? The evidence suggests to me that additional controls on the petroleum industry—to the extent that that is possible—would not be the solution. The only area left uncontrolled is the consumer or energy user segment of the energy market. The existing controls on the producing sector and distribution sector have led to perverse consequences and so, characteristically, the politicians now propose to extend controls to the consuming sector as well. This is the current plea for mandatory regulations and controls on energy users. Instead of deregulating the energy sector in order to allow prices to move to the higher equilibrium levels and hence encourage us all to use energy wisely with reference to our own specific circumstances, the government prefers to keep prices artificially low, encourage us to consume energy, and then step in to regulate still another portion of our daily lives and activities. Hence, the threat of jail sentences if you dare set your thermostat above sixty-five degrees or if you exceed the 55 mph speed limit.

I predict the consequences of mandated energy conservation will have impacts equal to or greater than the adverse consequences that have resulted from the government's meddling on the production and distribution side. For example, the December 1975 Cold Homes and Closed Factories Act mandated that all automobile manufacturers achieve an average of 18 miles per gallon in 1978, 19 mpg in 1979, 20 mpg in 1980 and 27.5 mpg for the cars they produce beginning in 1985. A noble goal, you might say, since it is eminently desirable to have automobiles that burn less gas per mile. But if available technology permitted the manufacturers to produce their current mix of cars and simultaneously achieve higher efficiency, they would do so automatically under the profit motive. No regulations would be required. The mandated mileage figures can be achieved only by reducing the size and weight of the automobile mix produced. Thus, the entire range of automobiles produced will shrink in weight and size by 1985.

Recall that except for a brief period after the Arab oil embargo began, small cars have not sold well in the United States. Americans have demonstrated by their individual actions in the free and open market that, given the choice, they want vans, station wagons, Cadillacs, Lincolns, Buicks, and Thunderbirds. Those so-called sensible Chevettes and Pintos, the Gremlins and the Pacers have been gathering dust in the dealer's storage lot. Rebates and other promotional devices have been used to try to move the merchandise on the low end of the market.

The American public has responded to the incentives provided by the low prices of gasoline and other refined products. Each individual makes his own choice between comfort and safety on the one hand and fuel economy on the other. If gasoline prices had not been kept low by government regulations, surely more of us would have shifted to smaller, more economical automobiles.

The demonstrated preference for large automobiles will not disappear simply because Congress mandates smaller cars through the 1985 mileage requirement. Hence, I predict the following consequences: First, the mileage standards will establish, in effect, an internal entitlements program for each manufacturer. By this I mean, in order to produce the relatively large automobile that the American public wants, each manufacturer will be forced to produce a very small automobile that the public does not want. Each small car produced will be the entitlement or ticket needed to produce a large car. In order to sell that small, unwanted car, the manufacturers will engage in a multi-dimension system of price discrimination. Since the cost of producing any automobile involves fixed costs and variable costs, the manufacturers will load all of the fixed costs of the entire operation on the large cars and will sell them for a premium. The smaller cars will be dumped on the market at prices very close to the marginal cost of producing them. Anyone who buys a large car will be forced to subsidize the person who buys the small car. In addition, Congress may place an excise tax on the large car.

Second, the competitive dumping of cars at the low end of the market will increase the concentration of the automobile manufacturing industry. Since the small autos will be sold below fully allocated costs, no firm will survive without a full line of large and small cars. Hence, the American Motors Corporation will either merge or fail. Foreign manufacturers who currently sell in the low end of the market will also be forced to merge, at least for distribution purposes, with manufacturers of larger cars. Honda and Datsun may manufacture large automobiles in Mexico in order to offer a full line and thus offset the losses on the smaller models.

As far as I know, these results have not been anticipated by the Congress, by President Ford when he signed the 1975 energy bill, or by the official bureaucracy. Perhaps you don't relish the idea of paying through the nose for a relatively large, safe, comfortable car in the near future. Maybe you should write to your congressman suggesting that the government control the prices of automobiles as well. Of course, if it did that it would create a shortage of the desirable large cars and a surplus of the undesirable small cars, other things being equal.

Just like natural gas, the price of the car you wanted would be low but you couldn't get it unless you had political influence. And all this in the interest of saving gasoline!

Wouldn't it make much more sense to deregulate the petroleum industry in order to let the price of gasoline rise to the social marginal cost? Then let each of us decide individually how much of our income we wanted to devote to automobile transportation. Let each of us decide if we wanted to drive fewer miles in a larger car or the same number of miles in a small car. Isn't it likely that mandatory conservation measures such as the mileage requirement will lead to unanticipated consequences that, in turn, will generate pressures for additional, extensive regulation and controls of previously private decisions? If the politicians believe that because we are one people, we should all have the thermostat at one setting, isn't it conceivable that at some not-too-distant date they could decide that because we are all one people, we should all drive one automobile, designed according to their specifications, of course?

Up to now I have confined my remarks to an appraisal of existing regulations in two principal areas: natural gas and crude oil. Space does not permit discussion of the effects of other energy control programs. Nor is it possible to anticipate which of the many Rube Goldberg arrangements proposed by the politicians has a chance to become the next phase of our so-called energy policy. Instead, I look to the record of past regulation in the energy field and I judge it to be an unqualified failure. Those regulations have encouraged consumption, discouraged production, and encouraged our dependence on foreign energy sources. The politicians admonish us to close ranks, pull together, think small, tighten our belts, and chop wood—and the best of all—don't be fuelish! But this attempt to divert our attention from the failures of their earlier cockamamie schemes just won't work. The politicians haven't solved a single problem in the energy field but they have created problems we need never have encountered in an unregulated, free economy. Their record is dismal. Yet they want us to trust them to extend and expand their controls.

I suggest, instead, we place our trust in the power of prayer. Let us all pray that Congress turns its attention from us to the OPEC nations. Let us pray that Congress tries to "help" and assist OPEC since, if history is any guide, the help of Congress would be the surest way to wreck the cartel.

Udall

Let me first touch on some areas of agreement, because some do exist. There is no question about the fact that we are in trouble. Bear in mind that until recently, crude oil was not regulated. Until the summer of 1971, when President Nixon put his price controls on, the oil industry was the most unregulated, freewheeling industry in the United States. It was completely unregulated until that point, except for oil import quotas. At that time Middle East oil was $1.00 a barrel, and United States oil was $3.85. So we put a lid on imports. This was a "drain-America-first" policy, which we instigated because the oil industry wanted it. If oil is as important as I think it is, we have certainly got to start talking about it in terms of national security. Today the Soviet Union's reserves are almost three times what ours are. If we are going to go ahead and pump America dry during the next fifteen to twenty years, we must realize that this course of action may have both economic and strategic consequences unless we can develop a substitute for oil in that time. In contrast to oil, natural gas has been under regulation. Natural gas consumption, natural gas sales, quadrupled between 1950 and 1970. There was a glut on the market. Some of the big oil companies are now going into interstate pipeline, under contracts that were made ten or fifteen years ago, at 7¢ per thousand cubic feet. At that time producers were trying to get rid of the gas. As for the argument that the wellhead price controls of the 1950s and 1960s held back the gas industry, I can only say that the industry was getting what the market would bear.

I don't like this Rube Goldberg system that has been created. It appears to be without basis in reason, but it is just an attempt to create equity among users and regions. If we try to have some kind of national energy policy, should prices be different in Maine and California? Are we going to gouge one region? We gouged New England for a long time with this oil import program, which was the one regulation we had. They kept it on too long, as I am sure both of us would agree.

There is another aspect of this situation that I do not like, and here again I agree with my colleague. Artificially low prices encourage consumption and waste, no question about it. But I now have to look at the other side of the coin. If you are talking about complete decontrol of natural gas (the controlled price is now 46¢ per thousand cubic feet) it will go to the free market price. We already have partial decontrol in both oil and natural gas for new discoveries made during the past two years. If you completely decontrol gas, it will go to the current market price of about $2.20. What you are suggesting, and let's be honest about it, is that we quadruple the gas bill of every homeowner in the United States. People back in the Middle West and East have been staggered by the fact that their gas bill has doubled in this very cold weather. Doubling prices is what you are talking about. We got ourselves into this predicament of shortages; that is the cause of all this. We overshot, we miscalculated and we are now in a situation of shortages. Crude oil will rise to the OPEC level, everything will rise to the OPEC level, because we are in a shortage situation. And if that happens, if you allow the free market to operate, the price of gasoline, of fuel oil, will double. To say tomorrow morning, "Decontrol—let the consumers pay," would make the people conserve. I have to agree with that. It would produce quite a conservation program, and probably deal a staggering blow to the economy too because it would cut out so much consumer purchasing power and create inflation. That bothers me. And it also bothers me that we would be giving enormous windfall profits to people who have proven reserves that they have already paid for. They have already amortized part of these reserves. Some oil and natural gas wells were discovered twenty years ago, and are still being pumped.

Now let's look at who benefits. The impact on the consumer is obvious. This is the reason Congress is wrestling with this problem. It is an awful problem that has no easy solution.

One-fifth of the natural gas going into the pipelines today—almost one-fifth—is provided by Exxon. If the proven reserves that they have are worth $200 billion now (I am just taking a figure out of the air) they might be worth, say, $800 million if we decontrol tomorrow morning. Now, when you talk about windfalls, that is what you are talking about.

Remember also that at the same time you are doubling the price to the consumer. That is the tough political issue with which Congress is now wrestling; if we decontrol we double the price to the consumer. I wish there were some easy solution. I wish that we had not made the miscalculations that we have discussed, and that we had stayed in a situation in which the free market would work. Unfortunately, the overwhelming reality is that our oil and gas supplies will continue to decline, despite what the price is. Although there may be marginal increases in production for a short period, the reality is that we are running out of petroleum. And because we are running out of a resource that is essential to our economic well-being and because no substitutes exist, the normal laws of economics, in the short run at least, do not operate equitably. We could have chaos in this country if we discontinued regulations abruptly. We are in deep trouble and conservation is the only way out. Conservation has to be the policy and it has to be consistent.

The official figures that they were using in 1974 were that our undiscovered resources were four, five, or some said, six times larger than the oil we have already discovered. Finally, under pressure from some people in Congress and some of us outside, the director of the Geologic Survey appointed a new team of young petroleum geologists who had no axes to grind. As a result of their research, the official estimates were dropped by 80 percent in 1975. Quite frankly, I think we have had our fling with optimism about technology, and optimism about developing substitutes for petroleum.

A lot of things look good on paper. However, I think we should be conservative in terms of our estimate of where we are, and of what resources we have and of what the alternatives are. I reiterate that we have overshot and we have gotten ourselves into an awful predicament. If we were not in so much trouble and returning rapidly to the free market were easier and less painful, I would favor such action. I am not for controls per se, but I see no way to accomplish the transition that we have to undergo during the next few years if we don't have some kind of controls so that we share the shortages equitably during this transition period. I just tend to think that when you get into the kind of trouble that we are in, which we got into gradually, we should get out gradually. And we are going to get out gradually by developing the alternatives. I think we are in agreement on this point. However, it is a long-haul proposition; it cannot be done in one fell swoop.

I am not pessimistic about our coping with this problem if we face up to reality and act. Let me be specific. I've been in New Mexico, I know that state. Although it is an energy-rich state, it may want to hold back some of its oil and maybe become the center of a petrochemical industry. Petroleum's highest and best use is not as a fuel. In fact, we are committing a serious offense against our future in burning it up. The overwhelming amount of your energy here in California, for example, for hot water and heating homes should come from solar energy. As for New Mexico's electric power—New Mexico is a coal-rich state—the people can provide adequately for their electrical needs through their coal resources. And they also will probably develop geothermal energy, wind power, and so on.

These are the kinds of solutions we need. The thing that is really shocking is the amount of waste involved in the use of energy in this country. We waste at least one-third of the energy that we use.

Johnson

There is pressure in some quarters for both vertical and horizontal divestiture of oil companies. Before you are tempted to yield to this pressure because you think an oil monopoly exists in the United States, I recommend that you look at the concentration ratios. At least twenty-five other industries are more concentrated than the petroleum-refining industry. What about profits? The rate of return on capital in the oil industry is only slightly above the average rate of return for all manufacturers. Yes, many of these firms are large, even huge. However, hugeness does not mean monopoly power.

The people on the front lines of professional football are also huge in their own way, but none of them seems to have monopoly power. On the contrary, they are fairly evenly matched and compete subject to certain rules which, if broken, occasion penalties that fall short of death or dismemberment. The analogy to the oil industry is compelling.

Divestiture of oil companies has recently been proposed: Should we allow oil companies to own alternative energy sources? In particular, should we allow them to own coal companies or to develop solar energy? As a Libertarian, I don't even like the question! I would have thought that Constitutional guarantees would preclude or at least discourage this sort of situation-specific re-arrangement of property rights. In my view, the oil companies' holdings of various energy sources are legal as long as the companies do not violate sections

1 and 2 of the Sherman Act or section 7 of the Clayton Act. If the oil companies are engaging in anticompetitive or monopolistic practices, let the Justice Department attend to it under the existing rules of the game. If not, let's keep Congress out of the practical issues of industrial organization.

Remember that oil companies possess a great deal of technical expertise. Most of the foreign oil fields in the world were developed with American technology by American corporations. This accumulated expertise in research, development, production, transportation, refining, and marketing is socially valuable as it is currently organized in individual corporate units. In particular, existing companies are well positioned to serve us by developing new technologies to meet our new wants. For example, at least one oil company is working on solar energy crystals and in recent months has improved efficiency of those units. In short, the argument for divestiture is based on populist political motives, not on economic evidence. Hence, I do not favor divestiture in the oil industry.

As far as tax policy is concerned, a high tax on energy would certainly move us up the demand curve and reduce dramatically the amount of energy we consume. But such a tax would have no effect, no stimulus on the production side. On the contrary, high taxes and "special" prices for oil versus new energy would signal producers—both existing and potential—that energy policy is uncertain. The government wants you to develop new energy sources but when you do, it will do to you exactly what it did to the oil and gas industry; when you develop a new source, the government will slap on price controls and taxes to extract your so-called windfall profits. Eventually the government will control the entire energy industry and will itself be the energy industry.

Mr. Udall's phrase, "If we deregulated, we'd have chaos," has a familiar ring to it. That's precisely what the chairman of the board of United Airlines said when he was confronted with the possibility that the CAB's authority would be reduced and the industry would be forced to engage in competitive conduct and performance. Politicians and big businessmen, including oil men, really don't like competition. In fact, few businessmen like competition because competition means that someone has the very real chance to fail.

Thornton Bradshaw, chairman of Atlantic Richfield, has recently proposed more regulation and more control of the energy industry. Why would an "oil baron" want more rather than fewer controls? Should he not favor deregulation if he is going to make as much money as Mr. Udall says all companies would make under deregulation? The answer is that Bradshaw wants the kind of controls that are government guarantees—really taxpayer guarantees—of high prices, secure investments, and stable markets. For example, if an oil company invests in expensive capital equipment designed to extract petroleum from oil shale and tar sands at relatively high costs, it would certainly be beneficial to have the United States government guarantee a minimum price for competing OPEC and domestic oil. If the prices of competing energy sources cannot fall by law, the new investment in high-cost processes will be protected.

Think clearly about who benefits from deregulation and who benefits from controls. The oil companies have much to gain from controls and, understandably, Bradshaw is now proposing that the government step in to fix the price of oil and expand its controls.

I suspect that many of Mr. Udall's concerns about deregulation and rising energy prices stem from his concern with equity issues—in particular, with the impact on the poor. But middle-income people will also be hurt by higher prices for natural gas and oil. I think we have to face a certain fact—it does make a difference whether the government or private industry produces oil and gas. The true social cost of the output may be the same but when the government is in control, $2 gas may be sold for 50¢. This looks like a bargain, but somebody has to pay the difference. For a change, instead of paying 50¢ directly for the gas and then making up the $1.50 through taxes, why not have users pay the full $2 directly and forget about taxes and subsidies? Why not be honest for a change instead of pretending that we are getting something for nothing or that we are getting a great bargain? If gas is worth $2 let's charge $2 for it across the board and then help the poor with direct income supplements.

Mr. Udall admits that we should have higher prices for natural gas, gasoline, and fuel oil in order to give us the incentive to conserve. But the purpose of this exercise is not conservation for its own sake; the social goal is to use resources wisely. And so prices should be set at the social marginal cost.

I understand and sympathize with Mr. Udall's worry that some people will not be able to pay those prices or that hardship will result. The concern is legitimate. Nevertheless, I point out that not everyone who will benefit from artificially low energy prices is poor. By federal definition, somewhere between 5 and 10 percent of the American people are poor. Note that to keep energy prices low to help this group, you also unintentionally help the other 90 or 95 percent who are not poor and who do not, in most views, deserve a subsidy through lower energy prices. If poverty is the problem, why doesn't the government solve the problem through a direct antipoverty program? Can it really be efficient to attack poverty through programs that rig the price of energy below the true cost for everyone?

Mr. Udall mentioned rationing, equitable sharing, and controls, as the three alternatives for dealing with shortages. To be professional: shortages mean there is not enough of a resource to go around at a given price. Scarcity is a different matter; all desirable goods are scarce but there are no shortages if the prices are allowed to adjust. We have shortages because we have prices controlled at levels below equilibrium levels. Thus, price controls cause shortages. The record of price controls is unblemished over the past two thousand years; they simply do not work efficiently. And prices set above the equilibrium level cause surpluses. The standard example here is the minimum wage; the good intentions of those favoring a minimum wage notwithstanding, minimum wages leave 30 to 40 percent of our unskilled teenagers without jobs.

According to Mr. Udall, the alternatives available for curing a shortage are rationing, equitable sharing, and controls for sharing. Why no mention of price? Why not let resources flow to their highest-valued uses in open, competitive markets? Let the prices rise and then compensate those who are hurt the most. Is it too much to expect that in a free society people should decide themselves the level at which they wish to set their thermostats? Is it unreasonable to suggest that individuals should be able to decide for themselves whether they want to drive a car that gets 10, 20, or 30 miles per gallon of gasoline?

Let's have the right price of energy in this country and then solve the poverty problem separately, through individual action or through whatever consensus action emerges. But let's not confuse the energy and the poverty problems by trying to solve them by a crude set of politically motivated controls that hamper or destroy the one effective mechanism we have for efficient resource allocation—the price system.

Note

1. Calvin T. Roush, Jr. Staff Report to the Federal Trade Commission, Bureau of Economics, *Effects of Federal Price and Allocation Regulations on the Petroleum Industry,* (Washington, D.C.: Govt. Printing Office, Dec. 1976), p. 56.

2

Private Corporations and Social Responsibility

Louis B. Lundborg and
Henry G. Manne

Louis B. Lundborg

It may seem a little strange to some of you and it may seem stranger as I go along, that I should be taking the affirmative side of this debate. I find myself feeling somewhat in the position of George Bernard Shaw when he was carrying out a difficult negotiation with Sam Goldwyn. Goldwyn wanted to make a motion picture out of one of Shaw's plays. Negotiations went on for days and days, getting nowhere. Finally Shaw turned to Goldwyn and said, "The trouble is, Mr. Goldwyn, you are interested only in art and I am interested only in money."

What do we mean by "corporate social responsibility"? If we mean that the corporation should be responsible for all the welfare, or that it should be solely responsible for the health and well-being of society, then I would agree with Professor Manne and there would be no more debate. There would be no room for debate. But if the issue is whether the corporation has any responsibility for society or, for example, if the issue is whether the sole responsibility of the corporation is simply to make a profit, then I think there is room for debate. To me the evidence is conclusive that the corporation does have to engage in activities intended to further the overall social interest of society. First, let me make one broad, general observation on the subject itself. Then, I am going to set forth six specific premises that will support, I hope, my affirmative position.

My general observation is that this concept of corporate social responsibility is not a fad. It is not a passing fashion, not a peripheral idea that can be swept under the rug in the face of apparently more urgent problems—inflation, unemployment, capital shortages, water shortages, fuel and energy crises. To me it is no less urgent than any of these; the alternative (the sixth of my premises), is something I hope we will never have to face.

What are my major premises? Briefly stated: Corporate social responsibility to me is inevitable, not just desirable; it is not something we should do, it is something we must do. We, meaning corporations, must engage in it (1) because it is completely consistent with the profit motive; (2) because corporations exist by public franchise which demands social responsibility; (3) because the public demands on which so-called legitimacy is based have so shifted, so expanded, that they can no longer be satisfied by production alone; (4) because the most

critical of our social problems grow out of the very existence of the corporation, (they are not the fault of the corporation, but they grow out of the same
environment that has brought the corporation into being); (5) because it is in
the interest of the corporation to further the health and well-being of society;
and (6) it is in the interest of a free society, the only society in which the
corporate form can exist, to maintain the vigorous private sector and not let that
private sector abdicate to government the solution of all our social problems.

Now, let us look at those six points one at a time.

First, the matter of profit. Of course, profit is the primary objective of the
corporation, just as the practice of medicine is the primary objective of a doctor
or the practice of law is the primary objective of a lawyer. But it is profit maximization over the long term and not the short term. There are many secondary
objectives that might seem to be in conflict with the short-term objectives of the
corporation but they are in fact essential to its long-term best interest. So the
practice of corporate social responsibility can be in the best long-range interest
of the corporation and consequently completely consistent with its profit
motive.

Second, corporations exist by public consent, by what we refer to as public
franchise. A corporation has no natural right to exist. It exists under laws. The
corporation must earn the right to exist and it must earn that right every single
day of its corporate life. If the corporation had no other reason to engage in
socially responsible practices, it would still have no choice; the public would
demand that it do so.

Third, the public expectations of the corporation on which the public
sufferance and franchise are based have shifted and expanded over a period of
time—very rapidly in recent times. Back through our history, we had so many
physical, material needs; we were critically short of everything and with the
development of the industrial revolution the miracle of production made it possible to produce most things that people needed. In the nineteenth and early
twentieth centuries, it took all of that productive capacity just to meet those
basic human needs; but all of a sudden (beginning in the thirties and coming
into full flower with World War II and the postwar expansion of industry) we
suddenly found ourselves with a productive capacity far beyond basic needs.
People in general, the great bulk of people, no longer had to worry about the
availability of adequate supplies to meet their basic needs and so they began to
think about other wants. We learn from Abraham Maslow's study that people
have a hierarchy of needs; as their more basic needs are met, they begin thinking
about their higher needs. Most people have reached that point. So the corporation no longer has quite the same magic based on its productive capacity and so
it is now looked to for other things. The public expectations—not only expectations from the corporations but expectations from all society of which the
corporation is a part—are in terms of needs other than simply the basic material
ones. We even saw the phenomenon during and immediately after World War II.

For one of the few times in our national industrial history the corporation was really a hero. It was generally conceded by the American public that this great productive machine of ours really helped to win the war, by implementing and equipping all the Western forces with materiel. It was a magnificent performance and even for a period after the war there was very little question about the so-called legitimacy of the corporation.

For most people this is no longer a concern. But about 10 percent of our population still remain below the poverty level and cannot meet even their basic material needs. For them there is no very great magic about the productive capacity of this corporate machine because they are not fully sharing. The disparity between those who have and those who have not is, if anything, greater today than in our earlier history. It is nobody's fault. It is certainly not the fault of the corporation. The corporation suffers along with the rest of society. So what is it that the public expects, in this enlarged expectation of the corporation? The public expects it to do right things largely at three basis levels: first, to produce and deliver its products and services at a quality and price that the market would find acceptable; second, to carry on corporate operations in a way that is fair to employees, fair to customers, fair to suppliers—to operate in a way that is not damaging in any way to the environment; third, to be aware of the problems of the total society and to do its share toward solving them.

My fourth point is that the greatest of all the social problems are those that have grown out of the industrial revolution of which the corporation has really been the engine. Every aspect of our lives, every aspect of society has been dominated by the operation of that great engine. Nobody sought to dominate society. Nobody that I know of in corporate life ever sought to dominate it. And yet the inevitable consequence has been that our whole way of life changed drastically when we moved off farms and away from small towns, into cities, into factories; moved from cottage labor, hand labor, into the impersonal assembly line, living in impersonal cities side by side. This meant a most drastic change in a whole way of life for the entire society. Life-styles as well as other kinds of styles, have been completely dominated by the product of the corporation. Food, clothing, transportation, entertainment, leisure activity of every kind have been dominated by the product of the corporation. Our environment, the air and the water that we use is inescapably affected by effluents; the noise factor in the environment is affected by industrial activity; traffic congestion is compounded by industrial concentration. Employment, including the employment and circumstances of the corporation's supplier, have been drastically affected and dominated by the operation of the corporation.

Fifth, the corporation itself is part of society and so it has a great self-interest in the condition of society. A corporation doesn't live in a vacuum. It doesn't live inside some kind of sealed capsule. If we want vitality in our markets, if we want people who can buy, if we want employees who are healthy, if we want employees who are trained, who are educated, if we want employees who are reliable, if we want employees who are free from drug addiction, if we do not want to have our operations eroded by crime, by violence, by vandalism, then we want to be concerned with the root causes of these problems.

Sixth, if we do not want government to assume total power over every phase of our lives, then we want to maintain a pluralistic society, not a mono-lithic society. We want a private sector, a voluntary cooperative society, to solve as many problems as it can and only in that kind of society the corporation, the private initiative profit-making corporation can exist. That is not only an obligation, it is an opportunity. If the corporation wants to leave to government all the decisions and all the issues that are going to set the stage for its own future it may be sounding its own death knell.

The corporation not only should but must pursue a course of social re-sponsibility—I might say a course of social responsiveness—because the public demands it as the price of its franchise, because the corporation's own self-interest demands it, and because the cause of a free society demands it. I think, in summation, it is really nonsense to debate whether a business has such a thing as a corporate social responsibility. Of course it has. It has an obligation to act responsibly in every sense of that word: to be aware of the consequences of its acts, the social consequences, the economic, the moral, the political consequences; to be aware of and so govern those acts that they will be benefi-cial, not harmful, to the community and to the broader society.

Henry G. Manne

I recall that I wrote my first professional publication on the subject of corporate social responsibility twenty-two years ago; sometimes I get the feeling that that is all I have been doing ever since. But the question used to be phrased a little differently. The term "corporate social responsibility" actually is somewhat voguish; twenty years ago there was a phrase, "corporate or business statesman-ship," and even before that "corporate citizenship." Flitting through much of this was another term once prominent in business schools, called "business morality."

What was it? Well, once upon a time there was a small haberdashery partner-ship. One day one partner says, "I keep reading in the paper and hearing about this 'business morality'; what are they talking about? What do they mean, 'business ethics'?" His partner says, "I'll give you an example. Suppose someone comes into the store, buys a new suit for $100, hands you a hundred-dollar-bill and walks out. As he walks out, you are rubbing the hundred-dollar-bill between your fingers and you notice that stuck to this hundred-dollar-bill is a second one. The question of business morality is: Do you tell your partner?"

We have come some way since that definition of business morality was popular, but I believe that the question of whether corporations should exercise social responsibility is and always has been a trick question. It is a trick question in the sense that it represents an illusion. It is based on a concept of a corporation that never did and never can exist. It is based on an epistemological error, the notion that a corporation is something that exists in and of itself.

Now it is very difficult, indeed almost impossible, for many people to grasp that there really is no such entity as a corporation. So if we do not start at the point of analyzing only the behavior, the constraints, the incentives of the individuals acting within the corporate picture, we will never understand anything about the subject.

If there is no such thing as a real corporate entity, then of course it cannot have a moral responsibility. There is a very old saying—I believe the phrase actually goes back to colonial American legal history—that a corporation is soulless. But it is very difficult to know how an entity without a soul is going to "save" itself by good works. Yet that is basically the argument of advocates of corporate social responsibility.

Clearly, the good faith proponents of corporate social responsibility really mean to refer to individual responsibility and morality and not to corporate morality. To refer to corporate morality is merely to confuse the issue, and I might add, significantly to confuse the public. But perhaps that is one of the reasons that we hear so much talk about corporate social responsibility from prominent corporate leaders and chief executive officers. It is so "convenient" after all for them to "forget" the distinction between themselves, and let us say, the shareholders of the corporation. They tend to identify themselves with the corporation and to talk about what they are really thinking of, their responsibility, their conscience, as being those of the corporation. And of course it is easier to assuage an uneasy conscience with someone else's money than with one's own.

The next illusion—and my talk is mainly about the illusions, myths, and ironies that plague this field—is that corporate social responsibility is something that only costs the corporation money. No one responsible in the field makes the mistake of assuming that pollution-control equipment, employee training, the whole works, do not cost money. But a great many make the incredible mistake of assuming that a corporation itself can bear a cost. Rubbish! There is no such animal as a corporation that can bear a cost. All costs get passed either back to suppliers (including laborers, investors, shareholders and bondholders) or forward to consumers, and we know that most of the cost of what is advocated as corporate social responsibility is passed along to consumers.

Still, this corporate social responsibility talk continues to sound plausible, because of another misconception about the nature of the corporation, and this has to do with the mode of its conception. An idea voiced quite clearly by Mr. Lundborg is that the corporation receives a franchise from the state and that it must continue to earn the right to retain that franchise and continue its existence day after day after day. Nothing, I suggest, could be further from the correct historical or economic notion of the corporation than that idea.

We get confused very often—and I must say that I find lawyers more guilty of this than almost anyone else—between the convenience of legal vocabulary and the reality of the world around us. For instance, everyone, at least a second-year law student, knows that corporations exist. Corporations even have rights under the Constitution of the United States. They cannot vote, but they are certain other rights that they do have—they can be sued, and they can sue people. But it doesn't follow that they must be people. All that follows is that for certain limited reasons of legal convenience we refer to the corporation as an individual. But to analyze the issue of corporate social responsibility that way can only lead you down a blind alley.

The question of whether there is a right of a corporation to exist is a fundamental question of any free society. It is fundamentally a question of the right of individuals freely to contract with one another in a way that does not harm third persons; that is all that is involved in a corporation.

I say that's all, but that doesn't mean that it's small. The number of individual contracts that go into making up the legal form that we call a corporate entity can be, I think, not merely in the millions, but in the billions. Corporations may represent contracts between two or three million shareholders, perhaps a million employees, transactions with tens of millions, even hundreds of millions of customers. So how can we say that it is not a thing in itself? It is difficult to change a popular mode of thinking, and yet I suggest to you that it is the only way you can understand this notion of a corporation.

What the corporation is, of course, is an enormous tribute to the ability of an unorganized and unregulated free market to organize the needs and wants of millions of individuals without the necessity of coercive interference by government. There is no significant feature or characteristic of a modern corporation as such that was ever given by government to the individuals involved.

In the early period of corporations, when their main purpose was running toll roads, bridges, wharves, and various public utilities, corporate charters were issued with a governmental gift technically called a "grant" of a monopoly franchise. Today, that situation represents a special kind of business regulation. It includes banks, insurance companies, electric power companies, railroads (when they have not been nationalized) airlines, things of that sort. The corporate form itself, as it developed in the nineteenth century, continued, as with "franchised" companies, to get an imprimatur by a special act of a state legislature. Later this was simplified to a stamp or seal of a government official. But corporations as a form of business organization had no significant contact with the government until politicians decided that they could increase their own political powers by establishing some hegemony over those corporations in the late nineteenth century. That was when we first began to hear talk about corporations existing at the grace or behest of the government.

Government and individuals in government are not, after all, differently motivated or constrained than individuals in business. In the same sense that a business person is trying to maximize the return on his investment, so people in government are trying to maximize their political power. Now that is a different notion than is taught in most civics courses where we hear that what they are trying to maximize is the interest of everybody else. Few mature and sophisticated citizens any longer buy that kind of cliche about our government. We know that individuals in government have their own interests, and we know what they are trying to do with them. We also know that they are constantly looking for the best vehicle they can for spreading and increasing their own power. And as they look around the private sector in a capitalist society, what is the most likely vehicle? It's our private corporations.

This government grab, done in myriad ways, is strangely aided by business leaders' inability to explain exactly what is going on. A recent network news program showed hearings in Washington on the question of whether one of the large oil companies was withholding natural gas from the market in hopes of getting higher prices later on. Or, as one senator said venomously, "just in the interest of trying to maximize profits." Clearly he was saying that they were doing something terribly, terribly, wrong.

And what was the answer from a top officer of one of the world's largest corporations? "We were only doing what was socially responsible." He was not about to get caught saying that he was trying to maximize profits, that the government had totally screwed up the natural gas business by price controls going back many years. Oh no, that would not go over well on television, so what he felt forced to say was, "We are just being socially responsible and trying to make sure that there is going to be gas later on." You can of course always be sure of future supplies in a market where you have freely fluctuating forward pricing, as we do with oil and gas. We witness such terrible confusion in these issues. You've gotten an interference in the marketplace starting off with price control of natural gas that leads to incredible shortages. But no government official can possibly afford to take the blame for that, and they know from recent experience that they cannot possibly get rid of the Federal Power Commission. So what do they do? Blame the private interests, blame the large corporations, and vilify the business leaders who, like it or not, are constrained by market forces to try to maximize profits, the very thing that serves consumers best.

The irony in all this grows because of the extent to which arguments about corporate social responsibility lend themselves to even greater government control. Let us assume for a moment, quite realistically, that one firm in an industry has received tremendous pressures, either threats of vandalism from hooligans, or perhaps more frightening threats from government hooligans called OSHA [Occupational Safety and Health Administration] or EEOC [Equal Employment Opportunity Commission] inspectors to do something termed "socially responsible." Who will be targeted as their most likely candidate? Is it going to be the new, small firm in the industry that might, because it is struggling to survive, do things that the community might not like? I don't think so. It's going to be the leader; the most visible firm in the industry will be the one targeted. That has happened on many occasions.

But what happens after that? As a very visible company, particularly if it is one that deals in large volume directly with the public, as, for instance, Coca Cola or the Bank of America, it is peculiarly vulnerable. Even a slight percentage turnoff by the public can be catastrophic to such a corporation in absolute dollar terms. So they tend to do what the terrorists are telling them to do.

Still, they cannot turn around and say to their shareholders and the public, "We knuckled under; we gave in." Oh no, they must convert that vice into a virtue, and there is a ready-made method for doing it. You pat yourself on the back, you put a halo over your head, and you say you are a very socially responsible company. And then you begin to notice something funny. Others in your industry are nearly as nice as you are, but they do not follow suit. If you do something profitable, you can be darn sure they will follow suit in a hurry. But when you do something that costs money and doesn't bring in more profit, they don't follow. They start getting more business, or their stock starts going up relative to yours, and you start to worry. Then what does the national executive say? "Well, obviously, we cannot have such irresponsible firms in our industry. It gives a bad name to all of us."

So the Washington representative runs off to the appropriate government agency or the appropriate committee on Capitol Hill and they tattle. They say, "Why, do you know that after we cleaned up our factory and no longer are putting all that gunk in the water, those so-and-so's are still doing it?" Now what is any self-respecting politician going to do? He is going to move as fast as he can to make sure that those irresponsible so-and-so's fall (or are pushed) into line. So the whole process almost naturally generates an increased amount of government regulation. Now, a belief in corporate social responsibility is not the only thing responsible for what is happening in government, but it has played a significant role, along with the inability of corporate leaders to cope with the problem of antibusiness attacks and their move to take the easy way out by regulating everyone into "socially responsible" behavior.

There are still further ironies, such as the proposal that corporations behave in a more socially responsible way, coming from fundamentally antibusiness activists. Ralph Nader and his followers are saying that fundamental government or social decisions about the allocation of resources, welfare, foreign trade, should now be made by the private executives and leaders of private corporations outside the constraint of market forces. I find that very strange. The very people that they vilify one moment under this rubric of corporate social responsibility are supposed to voluntarily assume the powers that normally go with being elected to government office.

Is there any reason to think that that is a good proposition? Are these people particularly qualified to decide what the foreign policy of this country should be, which countries we should trade with, which wars we should fight?

I suggest to you that they are not. Their special abilities and their comparative advantage lie in administering their corporations, making automobiles, making shirts, whatever it may be that the community demands in the marketplace. The further they stay out of government decision making, the better off we will all be.

To confuse a private responsibility with a government responsibility by suggesting that business leaders must have a hand in those government decisions is, I think, to say two things wrong. One, this confuses the concepts of private and public so that we can never straighten them out—yet we know that this is a fundamental difference on which most of our civil liberties are based. Second, it becomes all the more difficult to put the blame for most of our ills where it should be, on the government. The government officials just turn right around and say, "Why you know who got us into that war in Vietnam. It was those big companies forcing us to buy all those weapons we had to use."

One can go on and on with illustrations of the evils of ever paying tribute to such notions, or to the Ralph Naders of this world. The most overnoted social argument around is that to forestall government's taking over more power, business must do voluntarily what the political extortionists are demanding. That argument inevitably backfires. The good bicyclist pleasantly pedaling down a street knows, when a little dog comes running out of the yard yapping like crazy and snapping at his or her feet, not to start pedaling more furiously. The dog will only chase you more since the dog is not quite sure that it is succeeding in driving the thing away. As a result its courage grows and it chases even faster because it knows that it is getting the enemy out of its territory. That is exactly what we do to the consumer advocates of this world when we stand up and say, "All right, we will behave in a socially responsible way."

Over the years the list of things that opponents of business—and one can only call them opponents of business—have advocated as responsibilities of corporations has changed and varied so much that it is almost laughable to serious scholars in the field. There is no coherency to it at all. At one time it was "support universities," another time it was "support culture and the arts"; at another time it was "support the war effort"—whether that was a German corporation supporting the Nazi war effort or an American corporation supporting ours, the same arguments were made on both sides of the line. Now we are about to move into a new era, one even more frightening because it goes to the very heart of the corporate system. These are the proposals now increasingly heard to democratize the corporation, allowing representation of various community and employee groups on boards of directors.

This idea is well beyond the debate stage in Europe. The concept of co-determination was an early post-World War II phenomenon in Germany. Today in most large German corporations the requirement is that labor have 49 percent of the seats on the board of directors, and the debate going on right now is whether they should not have veto power. England seems to be moving rapidly in the same direction and a number of smaller industrial countries in Western Europe are in one or another stage of the same development.

Pointing to that development in Western Europe, and understanding little about it, Nader and many people in Washington today are saying that we must restructure the American corporation. Labor and other groups must be represented on the boards of directors. Many large corporations have already started giving special seats on the board to women and minority representatives. This will probably mean that companies will settle in private caucuses what they used to settle in the boardroom, and the board will become some sort of quaint public relations advisory group. We can see that as large corporations, the social leaders, begin to adopt these policies, it makes it that much easier for such practices to be mandated by law.

Another notion is that the corporation should not make so much money. There should be limits on profits. I do not know exactly what the limit is, but they should not be obscene, whatever an obscene profit is, and however you measure it. In the recent period in which we heard of obscene profits by the oil companies, the return was only measured against one previous year's profits and, therefore tells us nothing about the rate of return over a reasonable period of time in the industry. The business community never found the voice to explain to the public the complex way in which markets work or the complex function of the profit system. Increasingly, then, we find a certain tolerance, a certain willingness to say, "Why yes, I guess there has to be some limitation somewhere because we cannot allow profits to get, well, too great."

Three billion dollars a year is now being spent on employee safety regulation. Incidentally, that developed exactly as I described earlier. But how much safety has been purchased? None. There has been no significant diminution in the amount or intensity of employee accidents in American industry since the advent of OSHA. There is an insatiable appetite on the part of politicians for these things, but they can never be stopped with a defensive posture like that taken by the advocates of corporate social responsibility.

I think the public is right not to show much confidence in corporations that regualrly run to Washington, lobbying for tariff protection, for special licensing, for protection from competition in airline routes, in rates, in import quotas. They cry wolf, and I do not think anyone is going to trust them to be truly socially responsible. And even though the corporate social responsibility arguments usually begin as public relations, I think it is bad public relations.

Here is a case where business leaders have a moral responsibility. They should educate themselves as to how the free market system really functions, not as they are told by newspapers and politicians it is supposed to work. Then deal in a forthright straightforward fashion with the public and let them have it straight. There is no partnership possible between business and the government. There isn't any friendly supping with the devil unless you have an awfully long spoon.

Lundborg

In the real world there is a so-called legal model of what a corporation is. According to this model, the corporation is owned and controlled by its shareholders. However, today the shareholders are really investors, in-and-out investors, with very little continuing contact with the management and control of the corporation. The corporation is an entity with an existence of its own and quite properly so. In fact, I think that it is unrealistic to speak of the corporation as not having any existence of its own.

I think it would be unfortunate if we were left with the impression that what we call corporate social responsibility is simply a matter of obeying the law. Rather, social responsibility begins where the law leaves off, where the law ends—that is, in that area just beyond the law. There is nothing very virtuous about obeying the law. Society expects you to obey the law. But to be socially sensitive and responsible implies being able to see consequences of your acts. You must recognize that your acts may be perfectly legal and yet not be good public policy. This is the area of really sensitive public policy. It is the one that we should be talking about.

Corporate social responsibility is not a new term, a faddish word, a phrase for public relations. We used to talk about local companies as being good corporate citizens of the community. By and large, I think that most companies already try to live up to this standard. However, it is relatively easy to be a supporter of the United Fund who recognizes a little kid on crutches, but living up to this standard now is a more complex thing. Although a simpler standard might have been useful at one time, so many kinds of difficulties have been developing in just the last twenty to thirty years that our perspective must be much broader. In a very short period of time we have gone from being a predominantly rural, agricultural society to being a heavily urban one. This change has brought new dimensions to our problems, some of which are very subtle and hard to visualize. Therefore, it is not enough any longer to be a good citizen of the community. Most of those problems, but not all of them, tend to gravitate around the very large companies, the large industries, automobiles, steel, the very large aggregations. This is the reason that when talking about corporate social responsibility, we focus on the big companies. An important question that both large and small companies must answer is, "If profit maximization becomes inconsistent with corporate social responsibility, what should the corporation do?"

First of all, anything that is inconsistent with good social policy should be reexamined even if the result is an adverse impact on the final profits. Although profits are a corporation's primary objective, they should not be its sole objective. Many things that might, at least in the short run, increase profits have to be foregone because they would run counter to one or another kind of policy consideration. Important as profits are, they cannot be so overriding that all other considerations are discarded. It is easy to generalize and hard to be sure that a generalization will fit everything, but I do think that good public policy has to be brought into focus on a corporate judgment even at the expense of some part of the profit maximization. I think that this has occurred a thousand times, hundreds of thousands of times. Every corporation has, on some occasion, had to forgo profit maximization. There is nothing particularly mysterious about the process.

As for solutions, it seems to me that people give lip service to one preference and then act as though they really preferred something else. We say that we do not want so much government, and yet we continue either asking government to do more and more things or defaulting by doing nothing about resisting. I think that Professor Manne and I completely agree that we have much too much government in our lives and that it is something that we have not been able to stem. Governmental growth has been very rapid; it has lots of momentum behind it. Where we disagree is that I believe there might be some hope of resisting that trend, provided that we stop asking government to do things and take it upon ourselves through private voluntary or cooperative means to solve some of the problems. We go unnecessarily to government for programs, answers, and solutions. If we stopped doing this, we either might have to forgo entirely some solutions, leaving the problem to individual choice, or we might have to engage in some cooperative action. I have the feeling that if corporations as entities and through their executives would take a little more of an active role in solving some of society's problems, they might help to stem the growth of government.

Nevertheless, in some areas, such as pollution control, we have to have federal regulation of business. I think it is fundamental to this whole area but I do not really know how one factors it into a discussion of corporate social responsibility. We simply have to have the government impose the requirement on all of us. Now, as far as the automobile business goes, there is nothing particularly new about this course of action. For example, we have laws in almost every state that ban the sale of bald tires. Moreover, thousands of safety requirements govern the making of an automobile, and adding one more, a required pollution-control device, would not be a new departure in principle. Such a requirement would, of course, add one more element of cost, as Professor Manne pointed out.

He said that no corporation will actually bear such a cost, that it has to be borne by others. I do not take issue with this point. However, in contrast to Professor Manne, I believe that the corporation is the ideal vehicle through which the cost can be socialized and spread to the proper places. Professor Manne also spoke of the efforts and the pronouncements of the corporate sector, of the corporate leaders bringing upon themselves government intervention, government regulation, government harassment. I do not think that, for example, child labor laws were the result of that kind of corporate activity.

Manne

Mr. Lundborg mentioned the antitrust cases that were won on a defense of social responsibility and behavior on the part of the corporation. If that is a defense in antitrust cases, I believe that the antitrust bar would certainly welcome this knowledge. As best as I can tell from a careful perusal of the legal literature in that field, the Supreme Court has not yet recognized social responsibility as a defense. That good public relations may help one I have no doubt. All this talk about corporate responsibility makes one suspicious about what it really extends to. For example, why have banks not demanded of government authorities that they be permitted to pay interest on checking accounts? I might also point out the opposition that the banking community has given to the efforts of savings and loan associations simply to be able to issue checks. If we were really serious about corporate social responsibility, I do not think we would find so much running off to the government to get protection from competition. I think that we would find responsible members of these industries standing up and saying, "No, I will not take this ill-gotten gain any more; I am going to spill the beans to the public and the politicians and give up this business of using the public's money in checking accounts without paying any interest." But we do not hear such statements.

Child labor laws—I refer you to a most important book, *Capitalism and the Historian*, edited by the Nobel laureate, Friedrich Hayek, indicating that one of the earliest, truly socially desirable acts by modern business occurred when factory owners took children into factory employment. Why? Because farm labor, which was the only real alternative, meant early and brutish death for many children. Yet the corporations acted in pursuit of profit and not social responsibility. However, as the industrial revolution wore on, it became apparent that the children working in factories were competing with adults for jobs; as a result there developed this tremendous "social consciousness" about the evils of child labor.

Corporate social responsibility is not an accurate description of what we are discussing. I think the problem lies in the characterization of the issue and the manner in which the business community and the antibusiness community each addresses itself to this question. Much of this characterization by enemies of business simply reflects the fact that we are in another of the terrible, recurrent periods in American history in which the government is simply antibusiness. But I do not think that we have ever had a period in which we were quite so close to overwhelming the private sector as we are now. To put the problem in terms of corporate social responsibility is a semantic trap for blinding the public to what is really going on.

As to the issue of individual responsibility within a corporation—I expect individuals to hold a great variety of different values and moral preferences with different intensities of feeling. I would be surprised if I could not occasionally find individuals refusing to do things that superiors in corporate organizations insisted on their doing. During the Vietnam War I am quite sure that there must have been some Dow Chemical employees who left the company because it was making napalm. These are matters of individual judgment, of individual freedom that we want to protect in our society. Now, suppose that one of these individuals happens to be the chief executive officer of the corporation. Is the problem any different? As far as I am concerned, absolutely not. He makes decisions for whatever reasons—and accepts any costs that may be attached thereto.

Now, as to the issue of the corporation as an entity. The methodology with which you approach this question must be appropriate to the purpose of the question. If, for instance, you are talking about antitrust violations, clearly there is no point in talking about motivations of individuals within the corporation— that is, you can reach most of the goals of the antitrust laws by looking at the corporation as a single entity and not as an aggregate of owners and employees. But as soon as you begin talking about the moral issues, as soon as you begin talking about how corporations should behave, I believe that logic demands that you take a methodologically individualistic approach. As you do that, you find that issues become more tractable, that you begin to understand a great deal more, even though many people are involved—not merely the chief executive officer of a large publicly held corporation. Only by looking at all the interests of all the individuals can you begin to understand the total picture.

Efforts have to be made, with greater or lesser success, to allocate the costs of correcting "social" problems, particularly in the environmental field, as with air and water pollution.

Take one of our typical cases—an industry that not only has been allowed to exist as an environmental polluter but which was even solicited by the community in the first place to locate where it did. The community then begins to realize that the industry that had been welcomed is polluting the air or the water, and the community decides that this should be corrected. Everyone may agree that the air quality should be corrected, that no one should go on breathing the bad air. But the tough question is, "Who should pay the cost of this cleanliness?" Should it be borne entirely by the industry that was welcomed and sanctioned in the first place, or should the cost be borne somewhat as a social cost by the whole community? In a sense there is a little bit of this cost sharing in California, which voted a municipal bond financing mechanism under which industries may borrow money at low interest rates through bonds issued by the state for pollution control, thereby using the state's credit to lower the cost to the industry. Thus in a way all the taxpayers in California are helping to bear some of that cost. The industry bears the rest of the cost by paying such interest as it does pay, and then must pay the principal as well. A number of other efforts have been made to work out a proper formula for cost sharing. These things affect all society, and the costs should be borne broadly. But there is no absolute answer that fits everybody; the economists say, "There is no way to identify a social welfare function."

I want to emphasize that each of us does have a real responsibility to defend the rest of us and gain for us the benefits of a free market system before the government simply ruins everything. Unfortunately, there is no financial gain or profit in making that defense. Fundamentally, we face a free rider problem. Thus most business leaders would prefer such a defense to be made and to be successful, but no individual gains anything from his or her individual behavior, and everyone else gets a free ride. Well, that is the posture of our entire business community, almost to the last man and woman, and it does not leave me terribly optimistic about the survival of the free market system.

3

Should the Federal Communications Commission Be Abolished?

Ronald H. Coase and *Nicholas Johnson*

Ronald H. Coase

It is a great pleasure for me to be taking part in the debate about such an important agency as the Federal Communications Commission, even though its importance mainly consists in the harm it does. Above all, it is a pleasure to have such a talented, knowledgeable and sensitive opponent as Nicholas Johnson, a former member of the Federal Communications Commission, a status the broadcasting industry hopes he will retain. To have such an opponent, at any rate, guarantees that our debate will not be concerned with trivialities but will focus on really important issues.

I will argue that the Federal Communications Commission, which I will in future refer to as the FCC, should be abolished. The FCC regulates the telephone and telegraph industries but my concern in this debate will be the work of the FCC in controlling the use of the radio frequency spectrum.

We will not be concerned with whether the FCC is efficient in its administration of the radio frequency spectrum nor with whether it acts with speed, nor with whether it uses the right criteria in making its decisions. We all know that the FCC is inefficient, slow-moving and poorly, if not basely, motivated. As was said by James M. Landis, an advisor to President Kennedy in a report on the regulatory agencies:

> The Federal Communications Commission presents a somewhat extraordinary spectacle. Despite considerable technical excellence on the part of its staff, the Commission has drifted, vacillated and stalled in almost every major area. It seems incapable of policy planning, or disposing within a reasonable period of time, the business before it, of fashioning procedures that are effective to deal with its problems. The available evidence indicates that it more than any other agency has been susceptible to ex parte representations, and that it has been subservient, far too subservient, to the subcommittees on communications of the Congress, and their members. A strong suspicion also exists that far too great an influence is exercised over the Commission by the networks.[1]

Nor is there any evidence, I think, that the position has changed since this report was issued in 1960.

In 1965, Dr. H.H. Golden, when he was chief economist of the FCC, but expressing of course his personal views, stated that the procedures for choosing among competing applicants for the spectrum, were "ritualistic, formalistic, wasteful, and inefficient." And the next year a government committee, the Telecommunications Science Panel of the Commerce Technical Advisory Board, issued a report which told us, among other things, that the "domestic organizations which have the responsibility for the allocation and assignment of frequencies lack the tools needed to develop the objective analysis which must precede any logical and deliberative determination of the optimum."[2]

There has been no substantial change in recent years. I need only refer to an unimpeachable source, or at any rate, one not likely to be impeached by my opponent, the speechings and writings of Nicholas Johnson, much of which have been devoted to retailing the follies, and worse, of the FCC. However, I cannot refrain from quoting from the report of the House Oversight and Investigation Committee, which was issued in late 1976. The FCC, it tells us, has "been unduly wanting in vision and consistency of policy," "has been unduly influenced by representations and information furnished by the regulated industries," "has misallocated uses of the spectrum, subjecting it to wasteful and unproductive use."

I wouldn't wish to argue that all these criticisms of the FCC are correct but one does get the impression that the FCC has not been a howling success. Our debate therefore cannot be concerned with whether the FCC does its work well. It does not. But such a finding does not enable us to decide whether the FCC should be abolished. What has to be decided is whether such deficiencies are inevitable if an agency tries to perform the task assigned to the FCC and if we conclude that they are, as I personally believe, whether there is an alternative system which would work better.

Now what does the FCC do? It allocates bands of frequencies for use for particular purposes, it assigns frequencies to individual uses and regulates, in detail, the way in which the frequency can be used. The job is awesome in its range and complexity. We commonly think of the FCC as the agency which regulates sound and television broadcasting and it is, I understand, this activity which takes up the bulk of the time and thought of the FCC and its staff. But the vast majority of radio stations in the United States are not used for broadcasting. They are used by police, fire and highway departments, by forestry services, by airlines, taxicabs, buses and trucks, by telephone, pipeline, mining and construction companies, by oil companies, motion picture companies and many others besides. There can hardly be a business which does not add to the demand for radio frequencies.

How does the FCC come to know the uses which the radio frequencies might serve and how does it decide which of the various uses the radio frequencies will actually serve? The first question, "How does it learn of its uses?" is somewhat easier to answer than the second: "How does it choose?" If a government agency was presented with a warehouse full of steel, and was told to give it away, it would soon come to learn that there were people who wanted steel. In the same way, the FCC comes to know of demands for radio frequencies because businessmen, as well as industry associations, apply to the FCC and ask it to assign radio frequencies for the use of particular businesses or to allocate bands of radio frequencies for particular purposes. Through this process the FCC is able to learn something about the character of the demand for radio frequencies. But this does not, of course, tell the FCC which demands should be met, in those cases in which the demands in total exceed the total available spectrum. The agency with the warehouse full of steel might well be puzzled as to the criteria which it should use in deciding to whom to give the steel. The FCC faces a similarly impossible task. Of course the agency with the steel would presumably sell it to the highest bidder and would thus get rid of its problem, as well as the steel.

The basic question that I am raising in this debate is "Why do we not do the same with the radio frequency spectrum?" Why do we not sell the rights to use the various parts of the radio frequency spectrum to the highest bidder and thus eliminate the need for the FCC?

The easiest way, I think, to see what has been done in the case of the radio frequency spectrum is to imagine a situation in which a Federal Land Commission is established and the FLC, is given control over all the land in the United States and then has the task of disposing it to people without any charge. The position would then be that the land could be obtained from the FLC for nothing or it could not be obtained at all. In such a situation applications for land would pour into the FLC. Existing users, who have nothing to gain from disposing of their land to others, would resist any attempt to dispossess them of the land they were using. The excess of demand over the supply of land in many parts of the country would be enormous. The reasons given by the various claimants to justify their claim for the land would be persuasive, and sometimes even true. Lengthy hearings would be required to determine what use should be made of any piece of land. The purposes for which the land was required would have to be investigated; the character, competence, and financial qualifications of the various claimants would have to be discovered. Once a decision was made, continuing inspection would be needed to make sure that the way the land was used had not been changed without first having obtained permission from the FLC. The determination of what constituted a change in use would not be easy. The purely administrative problems faced by the FLC would be formidable. At the same time the pressures exerted on the FLC would be strong and unremitting. Business groups would oppose any change which would expose them to additional competition. Politicians would oppose any change which reduced the income of their constituents, or their own influence, or the income and influence of their political friends. No business would have any interest in economizing on the use of the land. Changes in land use would come about only with great difficulty and would largely depend on land becoming valueless in existing uses. The shortage of land undoubtedly would become a major economic problem and government action would be called for, once again to attempt to solve a problem which government action itself had created.

You may think my account of the consequences of establishing a FLC somewhat overdrawn, since there are in fact land use controls. No doubt they bring with them some of the consequences that I have described but there is nothing in land use control comparable to the range and detail of the regulation of the radio frequency spectrum exercised by the FCC. There is in fact no FLC. In the case of radio frequencies, no property rights can be acquired. No transfers between persons can take place without the permission of the FCC. Changes in the use of given frequencies also require permission and this is obtained with great difficulty. Thus major changes in the use of the radio frequency spectrum rarely occur. The situation which you now have is one in which the initial decision is very likely to be wrong and mistakes cannot easily be corrected.

When the potential uses of the radio frequency spectrum first became known, it was likened to the discovery of a new continent. The radio frequency spectrum is indeed commonly described as one of our important natural resources. But as we have seen, it is not treated in the same way as other natural resources. Just why it came to be handled in this very special way has never been adequately explained, at any rate never adequately explained to me. Mr. Justice Frankfurter thought the FCC was necessary because radio frequencies were scarce and therefore that someone had to choose who should use them—and many others have found this argument persuasive.

But of course, all resources are scarce and their use is normally allocated as a result of the working of the pricing system. Frank Stanton, then president of CBS, when asked whether broadcasting organizations should not be required to pay for the radio frequencies they used, could only reply that it was a novel idea. Apparently he was under the impression that CBS obtained the land, labor, and capital it used as a result of allocations from a series of federal commissions. Victor E. Cooley, chairman of the Special Advisory Committee on Telecommunications in 1958 said, "There are more applicants in some bands than there are frequencies. It is like seats at the box office when there are more people that want seats than there are seats. That being the case it seems to me essential that an organization be developed that can properly and in the public interest handle the whole thing." What Mr. Cooley did not seem to have considered was how it is that we're able to get along without a Federal Seating Commission.

I said at the outset that the present system for determining how the radio frequencies should be used is inefficient, inflexible, and subject to political and other pressures. I think we can now see why. The FCC cannot possibly have all the relevant information possessed by the managers of every business which uses or might use radio frequencies, to say nothing of the preferences of consumers for the goods and services in the production of which radio frequencies are used. Even to obtain a small part of this information must necessitate lengthy hearings. As the FCC's decisions involve the handing out of lucrative favors, it will not lack the attention of those anxious to see that the FCC makes the right decision, that is, one that serves a private interest, convenience, and necessity. All these problems would be avoided if only the rights to use the radio frequency spectrum were disposed of in the usual manner, by selling them. The result of not doing this is that "extraordinary spectacle," the FCC.

The picture which I have presented so far is however much too favorable to the FCC. Let us consider its most important function, the regulation of the broadcasting industry. As the FCC hands out the rights to use the spectrum, worth vast sums of money, without requiring any payment, the FCC is in fact engaged in a giveaway on a vast scale. Just what has been given away is revealed when a radio or television station is sold. Investigations have made it abundantly clear that most of what is paid for a radio or television station is in fact a payment for the right to broadcast. Or, if you like, payment for the right to use the spectrum. A recent study showed that in the last twenty-three years the amount paid for radio and television stations in the United States in sales approved by the FCC was over four billion dollars. This is not, of course, an accurate estimate of what has been given away. To get such an estimate it would be necessary to add the value of stations not sold in this period, which includes some of the most valuable properties, stations in New York, Chicago, and so on. Of course to be fair, it would be necessary to allow for double counting, since some stations will have been sold more than once. And then we would also have to deduct the value of the capital equipment of the stations. But what this figure of four billion, or rather more than four billion, indicates, I think, beyond any doubt is that the giveaway amounts to billions of dollars. I have termed this policy a poverty program for millionaires. Oddly, there has been very little criticism of this aspect of the FCC's work. It would seem that liberals are more interested in getting the government to regulate an industry than with discovering what it does when it regulates. No doubt my opponent will have a better explanation, or at any rate, one that sounds better.

I spoke earlier of the pressures put on the FCC to obtain these multimillion dollar handouts. But the pressures are not confined to this. FCC regulations can affect the competitive position of firms in the broadcasting industry. Existing firms attempt to obtain regulations which restrict the operation of their competitors. And they have not only attempted this, they have succeeded. FCC policies, like those of most regulatory agencies, seem designed to protect the industry that the agency is supposed to regulate, in this case commercial broadcasting. This it has done by, among other things, imposing regulations which have impeded the development of pay television and cable television. The restrictions on pay television have had what I consider to be a disastrous effect on the way the broadcasting industry operates. Under the present system, the only people who can pay for programs are advertisers. The broadcasting program market is a very extraordinary market from which the consumer is barred. To a very large extent the programs are a by-product of the selling process, the object of the program being to gather an audience for the commercials. The effect of such a motivation on the character of the programs broadcast is a large subject which I can only briefly discuss here. What one can say is this: of two audiences of equal size, the one that is most responsive to advertising will be preferred. In general, a larger audience will be preferred to a smaller audience, even though the larger audience is only mildly interested, and the smaller audience is intensely interested. The costs that can be incurred for a program are strictly limited. They are limited to the additional profits on the additional sales which result from the commercials, and this is a severe constraint. The result is that many people feel dissatisfied with the programs offered by commercial broadcasting and in this they are probably right.

A common complaint today is that the programs consist mainly of sex and violence. My opponent is engaged in a campaign to improve the situation by getting rid of the violence. Had it not been for the FCC we would certainly have had pay television today, and if people were willing to pay for the cost of alternative programs, they would have gotten them. This development has been prevented by the actions of the FCC. Newton Minow, a former chairman of the FCC, spoke of the output of the American broadcasting industry as a "vast wasteland." This may well be true but if so it's the FCC that laid it waste.

The final and in some ways most worrisome aspect of the present system of regulation by the FCC is the conflict which it sets up with the First Amendment. The situation which now exists in broadcasting is not essentially different from what it would be if a government commission was given the task of selecting those who were allowed to publish newspapers and periodicals in every city, town, and village in the United States. A suggestion that this should be done with regard to newspapers would be rejected out of hand as inconsistent with the First Amendment. Yet radio and television are a source of news and opinion comparable in importance to the press and in some respects more important. The FCC not only selects those who are allowed to broadcast but in granting and reviewing licenses it takes into account actual and proposed programming, or it claims to do so. Yet liberal opinion, so vociferous in its support of freedom from government regulation for newspapers, has largely ignored this problem— perhaps because to get rid of this threat to freedom of the press would mean abolishing the FCC. Nor are we talking about a danger which is altogether hypothetical. There have been cases of stations which have lost their licenses because their programs were regarded unfavorably by the FCC, although the number is not very large. With so many favors to give, it is to be expected that broadcasting managements would be responsive to some degree to the wishes of the FCC, although what the overall effect has been on programming is not easy to estimate. I suppose only the managements of radio and television stations are really in a position to say what it has been. But what is going on, what has been going on, is completely inconsistent with what we normally consider to be a basic freedom in the United States.

The FCC presents an "extraordinary spectacle" because we have created an extraordinary situation. A basic resource is given away, which necessitates having a body like the FCC to decide how it should be used. Of course, the task is an impossibly difficult one for anybody, and in consequence, the FCC drifts, vacillates and stalls. But the FCC is also a political body and it responds to pressures. In the case of broadcasting, by suppressing or restricting the development of competitors to commercial broadcasting, it has perpetuated something which is again extraordinary, a system in which the consumer cannot directly buy what he wants. This makes the market for broadcast programs quite different from any other market of which I know. It is a market from which the consumer is barred. No wonder there is dissatisfaction with the output of the broadcasting industry.

Given that the operators of broadcasting stations are licensed by the government, with the members of the commission appointed by the president, and their powers controlled by Congress, it is hardly surprising that the broadcasting industry, much more than the press, is responsive to the wishes of the president and the Congress and clearly seems to be more responsive than are, say, newspapers. The dangers posed to freedom of speech and of the press by the present system are real. All these problems could be eliminated in a very simple way, by abolishing the FCC and adopting the economic arrangements found in the rest of the American economic system.

Nicholas Johnson

When people used to ask me "Do you work for the FCC?" my response typically would be, "No, I work against the FCC!"

I don't mind taking the conservative position in favor of sustaining present institutions. My radical friend, Ronald Coase, seeks to destroy that which has been created and offers, I must say, very little in return for it.

I've often expressed a conservative view. I once wrote a speech called, "Why I'm a Conservative, or, For Whom Does the Bell Toil," which put forward some fifteen case studies in which the management of Bell had ingeniously come up with management policies that simultaneously lowered the rate of return to shareholders while increasing the rates paid by consumers. In fact, I have learned a great deal of my economics from Ronald Coase and Milton Friedman and those folks from Chicago and I find much of that quite compatible.

So I don't come in as a swinging advocate of more and more regulation wherever it can be imposed. But I do feel an obligation to treat the topic responsibly. Are we really going to abolish the FCC? That's the issue before us. There are a good many issues here that have not really been addressed.

What is wrong, after all, with our working together as a people? As a family, a school, a community, a nation, a state, we do together those things which we are incapable of doing as individuals. We have a socialistic public school system in this community, we have socialistic highways, we have a socialistic federal park system throughout California that's quite popular. We seem to feel that public schools and highways and libraries and national parks serve a useful purpose. And the ideological label that one might apply to them does not detract from the fact that we can move faster on those roads than we could if we had some free private enterprise system of toll roads.

The same principle applies to regulation. I am not in favor of regulation for regulation's sake. I would always opt for a marketplace solution if it could be found. The public interest is probably better served by having small firms that are capable of competing. It's rather hard to compete with an eight-hundred-pound gorilla. But having small firms that are capable of competing with one another, that will compete in price, technological innovations and consumer services is almost always better than oligopoly or monopoly subject to federal regulation.

Some things that we regulate, however, most people would agree ought to be regulated. We regulate who stops at the intersection; that seems to serve a useful purpose. We regulate what kinds of poisons and carcinogenic additives can be put in our food supply. We don't regulate them very stringently, but we have some regulations in that area. They are, by and large, publicly supported. We regulate the sale of hard drugs. There are arguments about the merits of making heroin available, as some countries do, to deal with the problem better than we do, but there is still widespread support in this country for the notion of limiting the sale of hard drugs. So what is this objection to the notion that we are going to regulate something?

It is important that we address the impact of broadcasting upon our lives. It's possible to overemphasize it, but it is almost never done. We tend to underemphasize it. This is an extraordinary industry in terms of its impact upon our society. I am not suggesting that it ought to be regulated just because it has this enormous impact, but we simply have to give it a lot of attention and care in terms of how we want to handle it. We don't want it to run rampant across our land doing the kinds of damage we can now document that it does. Some way must be developed for dealing with that. If we can do it through a free marketplace and competition, fine. That would be my first choice. But proposals to encourage that are all vociferously opposed by the broadcasting industry.

I really have tried to come up with solutions that would enable us to avoid as much government regulation as we have. What are some of those solutions?

I proposed that there be an opportunity for free access to radio and television stations so that all points of view in the society could be represented. The Supreme Court has said that First Amendment rights are not those of the broadcasters, they belong to the audience. We have a right to live in a country where all points of view have an opportunity to be expressed on the mass media. There is, in the language of the Court, no right of private censorship in a medium not open to all. And yet the broadcasters oppose the notion of free access. They even oppose the notion of paid access.

Fourteen United States senators at one point felt that because Richard Nixon had been on all three networks in prime time for about six weeks in a row that there ought to be some opportunity for an expression of a contrary point of view, to remind the people of the country that there is another branch of government called the Congress, to remind them that there are two parties in the nation. They went to the networks and said, "May we please have, just once, some time in prime time on all three networks to talk about this problem and our differences?" They said, "No, you can't." They said, "Well, O.K., how about just one network?" "No, sorry." So they went out and they tried to raise the money, five- and ten-dollar contributions from people all across the country. The fourteen senators went back to the networks. They said, "All right, now we understand your position. We don't like it but we understand it. We've raised the money. We'd like to have a half hour on one network to express our point of view." And the network said, "You fellows don't seem to understand. We are not going to put you on at all." If that's the way the networks of this country are treating United States senators, how do you suppose they treat ordinary citizens? That is a serious problem in democracy and it has to be dealt with.

The broadcasters oppose "dropping in" more VHF stations, which is perfectly feasible. We could have more television stations in this country. Broadcasters oppose that.

They oppose the prime time access rule that would free up more time for local stations from the networks.

They oppose the notion of lowering the power of stations, so you could have more stations.

They oppose virtually anything minority groups try to do, whether equal employment opportunity or less-racist programming stereotypes, or minority group ownership of stations. I think there is now maybe one television station that is owned by blacks.

They oppose the notion of public participation, the license renewal process, the renewals, the agreements, community ascertainment.

They oppose the notion of diversification of ownership, breaking up newspaper television-ownership that gives a monopoly to one person in the community to control what that community is going to hear about its problems. They oppose that.

They oppose cable television.

They oppose access channels on cable television.

They oppose pay television.

They oppose public broadcasting when it becomes competitive.

They oppose the notion of public service messages, free-speech messages.

They are even trying to tie up the videotaping business.

That's the real world, friends.

Whenever I have tried to break down regulations, that's the response I get from these free private enterprisers.

I have probably written as much or more about the FCC's inadequacies as Ronald Coase has. But I have yet to understand what the alternative it. He says there are limitations and inadequacies to the FCC. There are. That is clear. The record is there, and I helped to build it with dissenting opinions. But it does not necessarily flow from that that we abolish the institution.

There were many instances during the Nixon administration of abuse of governmental power. The Internal Revenue Service was used for political purposes, the FBI and the CIA. There are those who always wanted to abolish the IRS, and another group who wish to abolish the FBI and the CIA. But no one is seriously arguing that the FBI should be abolished because it is possible to abuse the power held by the FBI. No one is seriously arguing that the IRS ought to be abolished because its power was once abused by a president. You try to curb the abuses, you try to prevent them, but you do not abolish the agency. You try to make it better. That is what the National Citizens Committee for Broadcasting [NCCB] is doing. That is why we have that organization. Because we have to fight for our rights in this country. That is what democracy was always about.

Nobody ever said that government was going to hand it to us on a platter. Government provides the forum. Government gives you the chance, gives you the opportunity to be heard and present your case. The remedy is to bring citizen pressure to bear on these agencies. I think we have had some success with the NCCB.

I like a lot of what Ronald Coase said. I like it for two reasons. I do not like it for the reasons he put forth in this debate.

I was very much attracted to his argument in 1966 and 1967 when I first encountered his writings and first met and talked with him and tried to carry his message to the commissioners and staff, and the industry, and tried to get some of those ideas adopted. I think we need much more than we have had in this country, within industry as well as within government, of people saying, "Why do we have to do it that way?" As Robert Kennedy used to say, "Some people look around at things as they are and ask why. I dream of things that never were and ask why not." We need more people who ask, "Why not?"

Why can't we sell off the frequencies? Why do we have to have an FCC? What alternatives are there? Why do we have to go on doing it the way we always have? We need those kinds of people in universities, and organized religion, and companies, and government. And Professor Coase has provided that. I think that has been very constructive and healthy.

The second thing that I like about his proposal is that it does have a very real applicability in one area of FCC regulation, which he spoke of, and that is the allocation of frequencies for business use. The FCC solemnly goes about making decisions about which is the higher of two competing uses for a frequency. In one case it was a choice between a company that picked up milk at barns and delivered it to dairies and another company that was providing an artificial insemination service for cows. I used to look about for cases like this. They illustrate so well the folly of trying to make these decisions within a governmental agency.

In those circumstances it would be perfectly appropriate to say, "O.K., fellows, it's up for bids. How much is it worth to you?"

One of the aspects of the present system that Professor Coase did not discuss is that it throws a diseconomy into the equation when a business confronts a choice of using landline communications, microwave relay towers or cable to communicate between one point and another rather than business radios, citizens band, and so forth. When they make that economic decision, they are comparing the cost of building those microwave relay towers or laying all that cable or using frequency space which they get for free. And so they tend to opt in favor of use of frequencies when they really ought to be using a landline system. If you are communicating between two points, there is no reason you need to send out a signal in a 360° circle. You can just send it right down the line. But that's more expensive because you have to pay to do that and you don't have to pay to broadcast it.

I would not, however, support his land commission suggestion. Do we have in the regulation of land a system dissimilar from that which we have in broadcasting? You have private buying and selling of stations; you have private buying and selling of land. You have a zoning commission which determines how that land is going to be used, and you have a Federal Communications Commission that determines how the frequencies are going to be used. There are problems with zoning commissions, the same kind of problems you have with the FCC in getting competent people. You have people who are bought off; you have people who are not as bright as they ought to be; you often have an absence of intelligent planning. You have cities like Houston, Texas. But no one suggests that the solution is to abolish zoning commissions. The solution is to have more intelligent urban planning. How do we have more intelligent planning, citizens who care about their communities, who will attend zoning board meetings, participate in their process? That is the solution, and I would say the same thing applies to the FCC.

It is not the case that the FCC never reviews once it gives away the frequency. There is a review period every three years on these broadcast licenses.

As for comparative hearings, I would tend to agree with Professor Coase that they don't make much sense. But frankly, they also aren't used much anymore. Comparative hearings came about in the early days of television when there were three or four applicants for a single television frequency. The FCC would decide which of all the applicants was the best. They would compare things like how much studio space was going to be available. But suppose we did put the stations up for bid at that time. That still does not warrant the abolition of the FCC. Comparative hearings are a very small part of what the FCC does.

I would also tend to agree with him on pay television. We ought to have it. The broadcasters have stood in opposition to it. I'd like to see as much diversity as possible in this country. We do not want to hear only the approved point of view. We want people to have choice; we want to have video disks; we want to have pay; we want to have cable; we want to have commercial broadcasting; we want to have public broadcasting; we want to have listener-supported stations like those of Pacifica. Why not have as much range and choice as possible?

So what are we left with? We have an FCC which, if we are going to abolish it, has an enormous array of functions that will have to be performed by someone.

The FCC regulates the Communications Satellite Corporation, COMSAT, and participates in international deliberations in regard to where we are going to put satellites. It regulates the domestic satellite efforts.

It licenses people. Maybe you should not license people either. There are good arguments for not doing it. The state of California is now considering that with the new appointments of Governor Jerry Brown to the regulatory commissions. Maybe you should not be licensing beauticians, engineers, and so forth at all. But at the present time we do, and it is the FCC that does it for broadcasting. The FCC does not just award a license to a radio amateur. The FCC determines that this person, in addition to having the frequency, is qualified to operate the station, that people who work for commercial broadcasting stations are capable of operating the station without electrocuting the employees. That kind of testing, it seems to me, has proven to be useful in the marketplace.

The FCC licenses business radio; we have spoken of that.

The FCC provides "type acceptance" for equipment, doing safety checks on things like microwave ovens, citizens band radios, approving them in terms of technical ability. This is a major consumer protection and you can abolish it if you want, but you pay a pretty heavy price when you do and it seems to me that you have to think about that.

It does a direction-finding service in conjunction with the Coast Guard in finding lost planes, ships and so forth. It doesn't have to provide that service. You can do it commercially, I suspect, but if you are going to do that, it is another serious question that needs to be addressed. It cannot be tossed aside flippantly by saying that we are going to sell off the frequencies.

There is a world administrative radio conference that determines how frequencies are going to be allocated around the world, because radio waves have the nasty habit of not recognizing national boundaries. So somebody has to make those determinations. You have to address that question.

And, finally, we have the whole area of commercial broadcasting regulation to which Professor Coase has been addressing himself.

In sum, I would say that Professor Coase has demonstrated beyond any question of doubt his eloquence, his sense of humor and his brilliance. He has put forward a beguiling, intriguing and worthwhile idea which has perfect applicability in a very narrow area. If the FCC were to sponsor it, I would applaud that now as I have for the past ten years. But I think that Professor Coase has not sustained the case that the FCC should be abolished.

Coase

When you get down to it, it seems to me that what Mr. Johnson is saying is, "Yes, we need the FCC but, of course, we need a more intelligent FCC." Well, I cannot disagree that if it were intelligent enough, we would need the FCC, and the question we have to consider is, "Is it possible to imagine that the FCC would ever be intelligent enough?" I feel it could never be, for two reasons. One, the job is one that even a very intelligent commission could not perform satisfactorily. If we had a commission composed of seven Nicholas Johnsons, I still think the task would be one that would baffle such a commission. There is even a more important point—we are not going to get a commission which contains even one Nicholas Johnson again. That is the problem. The political system does not take kindly to a commission that uses its intelligence in an independent way. Now, Mr. Johnson stated a lot of harsh things about the broadcasting industry which I must say I think are often justified. The industry makes a parade of serving the public interest, but in fact it serves its own. And in this it has been supported by the FCC. The FCC has protected commercial broadcasting from competition, from, for example, competition from pay television and cable television. I therefore found much of what Mr. Johnson said about the broadcasting industry quite congenial. The only point that I would like to make is that without the political power which is possessed by the FCC, and its close connection with the president and Congress, the industry would not have been able to carry out successfully some of these rather unfortunate policies.

I would also like to deal with the suggestion which he has made, which I know is very dear to his heart, namely, that the situation might be improved if in addition to the existing pressure groups we add another one, these so-called public interest pressure groups (of the sort he represents). Now, I do agree with one point which Mr. Johnson did not make here but has made previously in his writings, namely, that it is not right to think of the FCC as just responding to pressures from the industry. It responds to all pressures. I think that is absolutely right. The question is whether we really need to add another pressure group. I am not as sanguine as he is about the introduction of another pressure group which, whatever its good intentions might be, is in fact likely to serve the interests of particular groups. I would agree that in dismantling the FCC one would have to have regard to its other functions, some of which could also be abolished, I might say, but some of which would have to be performed by someone.

Because I am sure that the FCC will not be requesting such assistance from me in the near future, let me now turn to the question of the costs—the money that people have to put out for the application process, the number of hearings, the trouble that they have to put up with from the FCC in order to acquire a license. Obviously if you are going to give away a large sum of money, people are going to incur a lot of expense in order to get it. In fact if they have to, they will incur almost the amount that they are going to get; in some proceedings you may reach that state. It is certainly true that in giving away facilities which are worth these vast sums of money not all the gain goes to the industry. Some goes to Washington lawyers.

My notion of pay television is that other people would be allowed to compete along with the advertisers. That is to say I do not mind some newspapers getting a large part of their money from advertisers but I want to preserve a situation in which they are allowed to obtain some of their money from subscribers, and if necessary, all of their money from subscribers.

I do not regard political advertising as any different from commercial advertising. It is not very truthful but regulation does more harm than good. I think one has to be a little bit careful when comparing our experience to foreign countries'. Take Britain, for example. Although it is true that there is no political advertising in Britain, the access of a politician to broadcasting facilities is controlled.

The arrangements are made by the main political parties and as a result it is more difficult in Britain for a party or an individual not affiliated with one of the major parties to put his views out on television. A notable example of this was in the period before the war when Winston Churchill was kept off the air.

I think that people get the impression that in Britain all is well simply because of this arrangement. But there may be members of a major party who are in fact expressing minority views and who, under the present system, could be kept off the air and in fact have been kept from broadcasting. I gave the example of Winston Churchill who never was allowed to attack the policy of appeasement of Hitler. I regard that as a very serious aspect of the way in which these things are handled in Britain.

Johnson

It is not necessary to add much. The issue really does turn on the point with which I concluded my opening remarks: What exactly is Professor Coase proposing?

Is he talking about what we might have done better from 1924 to 1927? Is he suggesting that we instantaneously abolish the FCC without thought as to what happens to its functions? Does he want a bill in Congress calling for the abolition of the FCC, period? Is that really what he is suggesting? If he is not, he is not talking about "abolishing" the FCC. Is he proposing a transition from where we are now to where we might be in some ideal world? If so, let's talk about the transition. How do we get there? That is always the problem, isn't it?

My first choice for any industry is an unregulated free marketplace. It is only my second choice that is regulated oligopoly. The only choice I find absolutely unacceptable is the one most American big businesses advocate, and that is unregulated oligopoly, unregulated monopoly. That solution is totally unacceptable.

If Professor Coase can create real marketplace competition, terrific. I hope he will tell us how he is going to do it. I have been trying for ten years—with shipping, telephone, broadcasting—and I cannot get the support of a single American businessman for the proposition.

I came to Washington operating on the assumption that business supports free private enterprise and government is made up of a bunch of socialists who try to regulate everybody. Was I in for a shock! What does business do when it comes to Washington? What does it ask for? Less regulation? Not on your life. Business wants to forbid foreign imports. That is what they wanted when I was maritime administrator. Our shipyards did not just want a tarriff on ships built in foreign countries. Instead they said, "We want no ships built in foreign countries that can be used in this country." Wouldn't it be great for General Motors if we actually forbade the importation of Datsuns and Volkswagens? That is what the shipyards wanted, and that is what the shipyards got. They absolutely forbade the operation in our domestic shipping trade of any ship made in other countries.

Business wants to participate in those socialistic governmental enterprises—mainly defense contracting—that are the most lucrative. That is the state socialism they are participating in.

When they get in trouble, do they apply their free private enterprise doctrine and say that those who do the best job in the marketplace will forge ahead and succeed and those who do not will fall by the wayside? Oh, no. They do not want welfare for the poor, but when they get in trouble, along comes the federal government and bails them out with welfare for the rich. Is that free private enterprise? Not on your life.

They want rates set at artificially high levels that the marketplace would never permit. That is what telephone rate regulation, natural gas regulation and airline regulation is all about. If you fly in the state of California on Pacific Southwest Airlines, you will fly for half the rate that you pay to go the same distance on the East Coast, where the CAB [Civil Aeronautics Board] is protecting your rights with an act written by the airlines.

That is the reason we have regulation! Business wants regulation. Who are the people now opposing the abolition of the CAB? The airlines. Who is opposed to the abolition of the FCC? The broadcasters who benefit from it. They want limitations on cable competition; they want to be able to violate the antitrust laws. So my major problem with Professor Coase's analysis is how we get there from here.

Let me now mention what the First Amendment is about in this area, according to the Supreme Court of the United States. The argument goes something like this. The government is selecting who gets to broadcast. There are people who would like to broadcast, who are financially and professionally qualified to do so, but who are forbidden to do so. If they engage in broadcasting, they not only risk going bankrupt, they also risk going to jail. There lies an enormous difference between newspapers and broadcast stations. A government sanction is given to those who broadcast in this country. They are selected by the government to engage in that function.

Suppose the government were to sit idly by and permit private censorship, which the Supreme Court has ruled to be unconstitutional—say, a decision by an advertiser that he does not want a particular program to air. The Supreme Court of the United States has said, "There is no right of private censorship in a medium not open to all." The government is saying, in effect, "Here in our public park we are all going to use soapboxes, but there are only three of them. Whoever gets the soapbox concession is going to determine who gets to have opinions in America." Now under that set of circumstances, according to the Supreme Court, the government must step in and say to the soapbox operator, "You may not exclude points of view from the airways. You have to give the people the right to live in a country where the full range and diversity of views occurs, because if you do not, you and we violate the First Amendment."

Notes

1. James M. Landis, *Report on Regulatory Agencies to the President-Elect,* Subcommittee on Administrative Practices and Procedure, Senate Committee on the Judiciary (Washington, D.C.: Government Printing Office, 1960), pp. 53–54.

2. Telecommunications Science Panel of the Commerce Technical Advisory Board, *Electromagnetic Spectrum Utilization—The Silent Crisis* (Washington, D.C.: Department of Commerce, 1966), p. 37.

4

Government Regulation and the Consumer

Alan B. Morrison and
Arthur A. Shenfield

Alan B. Morrison

The position I shall present in this debate is that more regulation, or as Mr. Shenfield would probably say, more interference with the free market system, is better in some situations, but not better in others and that there are situations in which less government regulation than we now have is a better idea.

The key, it seems to me, is "Will the marketplace perform its function, and if it won't perform its function, why won't it and will regulation help do the job a little better?" Questions such as whether the federal government or the state government or the city government ought to be in the business of regulation are beyond our present topic, so I'm not going to talk about them.

I think it's important to start by talking about what we mean by the term "consumer," or at least what I'm going to mean by it in this debate. Consumers you normally think of as people who buy products, buy services, use services. But in our discussion of government regulation, it seems to me to be fundamentally wrong to look just in terms of consumer pricing. After all, the consumer in that very narrow sense would do much better if we didn't have child labor laws and if we didn't have a minimum wage. But we have decided, for reasons apart from the economic well-being of the buyer of the goods and services, that those laws are desirable. So what I mean by the consumer is the consumer in the broader sense, for we all are consumers, and I will include it to mean the protection of not only the buyer, but the workers, the taxpayers and the citizenry in general. When we're talking about costs of the plant at U.S. Steel, located in Pittsburgh, Pennsylvania, we ought to think about the costs imposed on the citizens of Pittsburgh by the air pollution that comes out of the stacks of the plant's coke ovens. And it is not economically accurate to talk about the cost without talking about the cost imposed on the indirect consumers, the ones who have the smoke literally forced down their throats.

Well now, having said that, let's talk about an easy item. I think we would all agree that no one would be in favor of deregulation to the point where, for instance, the Pacific Telephone Company could go and charge whatever it wanted to. It's not acceptable. Nor would I say that anyone should be permitted to go to the courthouse here in San Diego and argue a case because he happened to want to argue a case and to take money for it. Nor would I suggest to you that anybody really is in favor of having drugs go on the market with no standards protecting the public, nothing at all except what the manufacturer wanted to do itself. We may argue about what those tests ought to be and what the conditions ought to be, but I don't think anybody is really in favor of having the day come back when anyone can go out and sell any kind of medicine they want without any kind of controls.

That gets us into our first very important area—health and safety. We also decided a long time ago that for the safety and protection of the public, the government gets in the business of regulating things like the police and the fire departments. Nobody would suggest that each person should go out and protect himself, if he thinks it's proper, by hiring his own police force or having his own neighborhood fire engine. So, we are trying to identify the areas in which we need protection, something more than we can do for ourselves. And I'd like to talk for a minute about drugs, not drugs that we worry about students using, but drugs that we think are going to be helpful to us and will improve our medical condition. Under the law as it now stands, for any new drug which you attempt to introduce, you have to prove two things: you have to prove (you, the manufacturer) that the drug is safe and, equally important, that it is effective. The law also requires that before any drug can be marketed, the manufacturer must go through a premarket clearance. It must submit evidence, proof of safety and efficacy, to the Food and Drug Administration. And after that, only after the FDA agrees that the drug is both safe and effective, can it go on the market.

Now, I think that's a good idea. I think it's a sensible, solid idea that after we have incidents like DES [diethylstilbestrol], in which the effects become known twenty years later, and when in fact it's been established that the drug was useless to prevent miscarriages, the one thing it was given for, that we ought to be very careful before we introduce unknown substances into human bodies. In my opinion there is far too much medicine going into the human body now that isn't useful for much of anything, and we don't need a lot more.

Recently there has been a great deal of emphasis on the controversy about saccharin. There are some facts that people ought to know about that. The first thing you read in the wonderful ads of (and I have to give them credit for the name of this organization) the Calorie Counting Council of America are things such as, "Well, you would have to have drunk eight hundred bottles of soda a day" (or whatever it is) the rest of your life, twelve hundred years, whatever— it doesn't really make any difference—"in order to have ingested the amount of saccharin that they fed those rats in the studies." That's absolutely true. The difficulty is that you can't do experiments any other way unless you're going to do them on human beings, because rats and mice, which are biologically about as close to human beings as we can get, don't live for more than a couple of years. And if you are going to give them any kind of an amount that's necessary, you've got to give it to them over a very short period of time.

Now the second important thing is, contrary to what you may have heard or read, that there is no such thing as the proposition that anything can give you cancer if you take enough of it. You are going to die of something else before you die of cancer, if the doctor keeps injecting water, for instance, into your body, or if you keep eating other kinds of natural foods. If you take enough of those things, you may die of something else, but you won't die of cancer. Indeed, in these very studies they injected comparable amounts of other substances into the same kind of rats and mice that were engaged in the saccharin studies, and none of them developed any cancer. They did develop other things, but they did not develop cancer.

And the third point is that you cannot determine a safe level for a drug, an agent, known to produce cancer in rats, mice, or human beings. So far no one has devised tests that would show what a safe level is. Nobody thinks that if you took one of those little packages of saccharin and put it on your cereal once in your life, you would contract cancer. But nobody knows that for sure, and nobody knows, once you've consumed that one lump, whether it's two, three, four, or what the number is, what is still safe.

Now Congress decided, and I think it is important to know that it was Congress's decision, made back in the 1950s, "That's enough for us. If rats and mice get cancer, we don't want to put those kinds of drugs in human beings. We think that there are enough risks in the world without doing that." I think that decision is right. I think it makes sense. But if it's going to be changed, we ought to understand that what we are doing is putting a lot of drugs on the market which may be beneficial, but they may not. We've found far too often that the tests used by manufacturers turn out to be not quite as well designed as they were supposed to be. They turn out to have neglected some things, and they turn out not to have told the whole story in a lot of cases. So I'm rather skeptical about a lot of this evidence. I suppose I would be less skeptical if the manufacturers were less unwilling to divulge the test data—how many animals they tested, under what circumstances and conditions. But I have a rather strong skepticism about it, and therefore I am concerned very much about the introduction of more drugs that I don't think are probably terribly effective to begin with.

Now, as with drugs, a few years ago Congress passed laws on toy safety. They said that the Consumer Products Safety Commission could ban toys that were unsafe: little toy ovens that heat up to 250 degrees, toys with very sharp springs or electrical wires that were giving electric shocks to children, or toys that had sharp, protruding objects. Milton Friedman may be a great economist, and he may believe in the law of supply and demand, but you can't tell me that little children who are buying toys really ought to be governed by that kind of marketplace mechanism, particularly given the influence that television has on the buying habits of most young people, if not their elders.

Now another area that I am sure we are going to hear about in this debate, and what a terrible thing it is, interfering with the free market system, is the Occupational Safety and Health Administration or OSHA as it is called. OSHA is the organization within the Department of Labor that sets health and safety standards, not for consumers, but for workers. It ensures that workers have a safe place in which to work, and, of course, it does increase the cost to the consumer. There is no question about that. But Congress has decided that that's a benefit the consumer has to pay for, that health is too important an item for the workers to have bargained away by their representatives or taken away from them by management. For one thing, a lot of the health problems are long term, produced by chemicals in the workplace, and they are not the kind of health problems we're worried about in the short term. You don't see your bladder becoming infected with chemicals that are going to cause cancer twenty or thirty years from now. That doesn't take place immediately. Workers don't know about it. Indeed, in many of these occupational cancers that have developed, there was enormous difficulty even establishing that there was a problem, because workers would simply die, or move off to other places, and the health records weren't collected. It was only many years after the fact that people suddenly began to realize that chemicals which were very carelessly handled in the workplace were producing very serious diseases not only for workers but for their families. In some cases, for instance asbestos, the fibers would get on the clothing of these workers, they would take them home and their wives and children would end up with the same kind of occupational cancer.

Another reason that the federal government was thought appropriate to come in and protect the workers was that the group that would normally, we think, protect the workers—their collective bargaining labor unit—simply doesn't have the technical expertise to be able to do this kind of work. Very few unions can have on their staff scientists of the type needed to protect the workers. Moreover, the union officials who bargain on behalf of the union are in general not down on the front lines anymore. They graduated from the factory up to the front office, and the sense of immediacy about working conditions is much less important to them than it is to the workers out on the line, and the workers out on the line also think often only in terms of the paycheck.

Now, the manufacturers are always saying, "Well, it's going to be a disaster, you're going to put the plants out of business and we won't be able to do anything." That's what they said about polyvinyl chloride. That's the chemical which was used as a synthetic particularly in a number of factories where tires were made. And an enormous number of workers came down with a very rare form of bladder cancer. The chemical was almost immediately taken off the market, suspended, very strict conditions were imposed, and during the course of the proceedings all of the industries said, "We're going to have to go out of business, you're not going to be able to handle this the way you said you were going to handle it and we're going to have to shut down. There's going to be massive unemployment and lots of businesses are going to go under." Well, a year later, somehow American ingenuity came to the forefront, and all these companies were still in business except for a couple that were very inefficient to begin with. And so I would say that I have a great deal of faith in the American free enterprise system and its ability to come up with solutions when they are necessary.

The last reason I think it's important that there be occupational safety standards is that there will be some people, some companies that might want to protect the worker. But realizing that it costs money to do so, they are unwilling to put themselves at a competitive disadvantage regarding the other workers, the other industries, other companies. And thus for that reason, they would be reluctant to go in and do what is right. But if they are required to do so, if the requirement is imposed across the board, there will be none of that kind of discrimination.

Now, OSHA has an abysmal record so far. In more than five years it's only had proceedings involving fifteen chemicals and the only reason it had any of those was that it was sued and told it had to do something about these chemicals. What it had been spending time on was worrying about things like ladders—you probably heard the story because it's the one opponents of the agency are talking about all the time, about the provision for putting toilets on ranches out in the middle of the desert someplace. And the reason that OSHA is worrying about that is plain old politics. During 1972 the person in the Labor Department who was supposed to be in charge of all that wrote a memo to the White House saying, "Don't worry about it, we'll take care of it; we'll be sure that no new standards come out before the election because we realize that our contributors and supporters wouldn't like it." That kind of attitude has been carried forward ever since, and it has shown that there's got to be change, there's got to be better regulation, not that there has to be no regulation at all.

Outside the area of health and safety, the questions become somewhat different. Let us look at the areas where there is economic regulation of one kind. For instance, the Federal Trade Commission, among other agencies throughout all of the government in this country, regulates false and deceptive advertising. Is that a bad idea? Should we just allow people to go out and lie, steal, cheat, tell people that things are true when they're not true? Should we rely on industry, or isn't it a better idea to have somebody protecting the public? And if they're going to protect the public, isn't it a better idea to do something before all of the damage takes place instead of afterwards?

Look at what happened to workers' pensions. For years everyone had said, "That's a free market; there's a bargaining situation going on. Let's let the workers and managers bargain together, and they will come up with a fair pension plan." Well, it didn't happen. The pension plans that resulted from a bargaining process led to a situation in which companies would merge and the pension plan of the company that went out of business would itself go out of business at the same time. Employees could get fired and lose all their pension rights. Vesting provisions, that is, the right to get your money out even after you left, were very onerous. You could contribute for ten, fifteen, or twenty years and not get a nickel back. The bosses of the unions generally got better pension plans than their members did. The members had no idea what was in the plan; they had no control over their investment; pension plans went broke. So Congress finally put down its foot and said, "The free enterprise system hasn't worked. The marketplace doesn't work, and we are going to insist that certain disclosures be made." I must confess that the people who wrote that law obviously didn't have English as their mother tongue. They also overregulated some areas and required too much paperwork, and it may even be that they have badly regulated it, but they have probably necessarily regulated an area that needs to be regulated.

I did say that I was going to talk about the necessity for less regulation and I want to do that briefly now. The federal Civil Aeronautics Board [CAB] regulates price and service conditions, not the safety conditions, of the airline industry. It has for too long clamped lids on conditions of fare structure and market entry in a way that has stifled competition. While I think the CAB is still necessary to protect people from unscrupulous practices by airlines in things such as ticketing, reservations, baggage handling and other things, it certainly doesn't need to be in the business of telling one airline how much it can charge you or me when we fly from one coast to the other. The General Accounting Office, [GAO] an arm of the Congress, recently concluded a study in which it determined that the fares in the United States were between 22 percent and 52 percent higher than they would have been in the absence of CAB regulation. It also found that the excess charges to the customers have been between $1.4 and $1.8 billion a year from 1969 to 1974 because of CAB regulating of prices, and that if you include in the savings the additional revenue generated, the additional passengers who would have flown if the fares were lower instead of higher, the figures would be between $1.8 and $2.5 billion a year. In addition, the airlines would have had increased revenues of $500 million a year, and they would have earned 12 percent return on their investment instead of the much lower figure which they actually earned. Now there would be some cost to deregulation. GAO suggests that one of the first things that might happen is there might not be any first-class service on airlines anymore. Kind of an interesting phenomenon that the government should produce first-class service and the free enterprise system should not! I don't think that you have to agree with that particular conclusion to discern that in fact there is going to be change. The study also suggested that food might not be served on every flight. For those of us who travel from time to time that's probably a blessing, rather than a penalty. There may be less room, feet may be a little closer together. There may be some reduction in service. Maybe. No one really seems to know.

All kinds of objections are going to be raised: "You're going to cut out service to a small community here, a small community there." That kind of objection seems to me to be directed not at whether deregulation is proper, but whether we ought to replace what is subsidy now—that is, have everybody pay more for airfare—with another kind of subsidy which the members of Congress, and this is probably why they don't like it, are going to have to sit down and vote for. They're going to have to vote—it's going to say, "Subsidy for San Diego-Los Angeles route, $16 million and there's going to be a recorded vote on that. Now you can understand why members of Congress would much rather have it hidden than have to vote on it, much the same as they didn't like to have to vote on their pay increases. But that's a different question from whether deregulation makes sense.

Now who opposes deregulation? Is Ralph Nader opposed to deregulation? Does the CAB oppose deregulation? Does the President of the United States oppose deregulation? Or do the airlines oppose deregulation? Well, I'll give you one big guess. The airlines, and they oppose it because they like the present situation. They are all afraid that one of them, in the spirit of the free enterprise system, might go broke and they might actually have to go out of business, and they might have to change the way they're doing things. And they don't like that. They are afraid of the future.

Let me mention another kind of regulation that those who talk about government regulation the most seem to overlook. That's the tax laws. There are provisions in the tax laws for percentage depletion, which means that mining companies can take more tax write-offs than it actually costs them to mine the mineral. There is accelerated depreciation, which lets real estate investors write off the cost of the buildings faster than they are actually depreciating. There are investment credits which regulate manufacturers in the sense of encouraging them to do one thing or another. And there is the subsidy for municipal bonds which in effect pays people to buy municipal bonds which they wouldn't buy otherwise. Now many of the people who talk about the evils of government regulation would be the first to jump on the bandwagon to defend those provisions of the tax laws which are in reality direct subsidies, or a kind of government interference with the marketplace. So there really aren't good regulations or bad regulations because they are regulations, but because they do or do not do something which is useful for the public. There is not going to be absence of regulation any time in the near future, so we'd better learn to live with it. And if we live with it, we'd better be sure that we have both sides heard on the question.

Now what do we mean by regulation? Some things are obvious. Somebody tells you what you've got to charge for your product, what you've got to have in your product, or that you can't sell your drugs. That's obviously a regulation. Is it also regulation if a few manufacturers get together and agree to charge the same price for bread and eliminate the free enterprise system that way, and the government sues under antitrust laws which say that you can't get together and agree on price? Is that what anybody means by government regulation because it happens to be the Justice Department that sues? I don't think we mean that.

What about regulation of a profession? Is it regulation of the profession when the lawyers all get together and agree to fix prices? Is it regulation of a profession when the lawyers all get together and agree not to advertise, to prohibit people from advertising? Is it regulation when the lawyers all decide that they're not going to admit lawyers from out of state unless they take the bar exam? Is it regulation when lawyers decide whether life insurance salesmen can tell people the consequences of life insurance policies and the tax effects of them, or when accountants try to help you with your tax return?

Is all this regulation? Well, yes, it's regulation. But it's a different kind of regulation. It's called self-regulation. It's self-regulation, but it's self-regulation that affects lots of other people besides the group that's being self-regulated. From the point of view of the regulators in that situation, the bar, for example, it's the best of all possible worlds. You get to decide who's going to compete with you, you get to decide what the conditions of the market are, you get to decide everything in the world that you want.

There's only one trouble—you forget about affecting the public interest. And if this kind of regulation is going to continue, it's got to continue in a different form in which there is a less-unacceptable solution. Either that, or it's got to go to total freedom. I don't think many people here are in favor of allowing everybody to go into a federal court here and say, "I can try a case, or I can argue an appeal." Maybe that wouldn't be such a bad idea. But if we are not going to do that, then we probably ought to say that there's got to be regulation. And it may look like more regulation than we have now, but that's only because the regulatory authorities would be wearing a public cloak instead of the cloak of the bar.

I suppose that you have heard of the proposal that our organization, Public Citizen, is in favor of, and that is the proposal to subject the 500 largest corporations in the country to more detailed rules regarding their activities, the so-called Federal Chartering Proposal. It would, among other things, extend antitrust protection to break up companies which control large shares of the market simply because they have control over the market. It would require additional disclosures for the benefit of shareholders, taxpayers, and citizens who live in the area in which the corporation operates. It would require that corporate elections be democratic, and that the corporate boards be accountable to the citizens and the shareholders. Now, is this regulation, or is this really the restoration of the free enterprise system, allowing democratic ideals to work for it? It seems to me that it depends on how you look at it and that the word regulation is not a neutral question but is a question of where you start from. If you begin back at first principle where there were no monopolies, where there were no controls of these kinds of industries in that way, you would have seen a gradual movement forward and an accumulation of power that is contrary to what we have thought of as our free enterprise system.

Now, if you think that these big companies are in fact regulating themselves because they are almost a government unto themselves, then you look at what they are doing themselves as regulation in a kind of governmental way. But if in fact you think that they are doing something different, then any imposition would be an imposition of government on top of that.

So it's not a neutral concept. You can't decide, looking at the present alone, whether something is more regulation or less regulation. The question is, "Does it help to restore the free enterprise system, at least insofar as it is capable of operating?" The message I want to leave with you is that there is no reflex answer to the question of whether more regulation is better or not. The question we really ought to ask is, "Has the marketplace worked? Will it continue to work?" If not, then regulation may be required. But if you are going to regulate, be sure that you hear both sides of the question.

Arthur A. Shenfield

I was under the impression that Mr. Morrison would have demonstrated to you the need for more regulation in the United States for the protection of the consumer or for the advancement of his or her interests. But you have noticed that until almost his last few words, he was concerned essentially with saying the following: First, there are some fields where regulation is not necessary; second, there are some fields where regulation may even be harmful; but third, there are many fields where existing regulation is desirable and justified. True, it was his third part that received most emphasis, but that did not amount to saying that more regulation was needed. Only in the case of OSHA did he, for a fleeting moment, suggest to you that there should be more, or as he styled it, better, regulation, and that because OSHA had been playing politics, a very revealing statement.

Later, when he came to the question of the revision of corporation law and perhaps the entrustment of corporation law to the federal power instead of to the state powers, he did not tell us whether that would be more regulation or not.

Therefore I must put to you that practically no case has been presented for more regulation. However, I do not propose to rest my case on that account because I believe that the interests of the American consumer, indeed the interests of the whole American nation, call for less regulation, indeed much less. Before I develop that case in some detail, let me paint a few broad strokes on the canvas.

I know what regulation does to an economy. I hail from a country and belong to a nation, which could in the fairly recent past, legitimately claim to be number one in the world in point of political and economic expertise. Britain could then claim to be the teacher of the whole world in the arts of political and economic management. Her parliament commanded the admiration of the whole free world, and was copied by numerous nations or states which became independent in recent times. It was Britain which handed down a legacy of political ideology to Americans, the roots of whose success are to be found in Magna Carta, the Habeas Corpus Act of 1679, and the Bill of Rights of 1689.

The British nation was famous for its economists, for it produced most of the classical economists as well as a sizable number of Europe's great political philosophers. Yet, as you all know and I have with regret to acknowledge, that once-great nation has been suffocating itself for a whole generation and more. And it has been suffocating itself precisely through its deplorable decision, or rather series of decisions, taken very gradually over the past eighty years, to embrace the processes of governmental regulation and intervention in all its economic and social affairs. It has entrusted its government with the task of solving its economic and social problems, in which task its governments, a whole succession of them of more than one color, have failed miserably.

This is a vital lesson for the American people because, as is clear not only to a visiting Englishman but also to a growing number of Americans, the United States is treading the same path. At an accelerating speed the United States is suffocating itself with the same devices, though usually in different form and with different mechanisms, as have the British. That America has not yet gone as far down that road as Britain may blind many to the direction in which it is heading. Despite the differences in form and mechanism, America's present destination is precisely the same position to which the British have allowed themselves to descend. There are two indexes, British and American, which prove it up to the hilt, and which Americans had better read, mark, learn, and inwardly digest for the benefit of their future.

In the past twenty years, of all the major industrial countries of the West, the two with the lowest average annual growth in their economies are Britain and the United States. Of all the major Western industrial countries, the two in which, over the last decade, the rate of new investment is lowest are Britain and the United States. And for the same reason. The fact that the United States is still in economic terms the most advanced and most affluent country in the world merely indicates what a marvelous legacy the Americans of today have inherited from their free enterprise ancestors. But that legacy is being dissipated, and the dissipation arises from the growing attachment of millions of Americans to the idea of regulation and, of course, governmental intervention.

Now let me proceed to detail. Mr. Morrison, in his defense of existing regulation, tells us that what the Food and Drug Administration does is excellent, that you could not have anything better. When the FDA was established in 1906, its task was to test drugs for safety, and food processing and selling for hygiene. I do not need to argue here whether that is a proper function of government or not; it is possible to mount a respectable case against it. However, for the purposes of this debate I shall accept it. Hence I shall not object in principle to what the FDA did about drugs until a little more than a decade ago, when a sea change was imposed upon it. It was a change that Mr. Morrison applauds, namely that instead of merely seeing to it that unsafe drugs do not pass to the market, the FDA was authorized by Congress to consider whether drugs were effective or not.

Now whether or not it is a proper function of government to deal with the safety of drugs, it is in no way a proper function of government, or of any arm of government, to see whether anything you buy is effective or not. That is your business, and yours alone; except that in the case of drugs most people will be wise enough to see to their business by taking the advice to their doctors. If a drug is safe, it is no business of the government to stop you from buying it even if it is a complete waste of your money.

As it happens, the FDA is no better than you are in deciding whether it is a waste of money or not, because the rules are of an inflexible character, which is just what is inappropriate in judging effectiveness. In fact, so harmful has this regulation been, that it has been conclusively shown in academic studies that whereas when the FDA was concerned only with safety, the American drug industry became the greatest and most innovative in the world, with vast consequent benefits not only to the American economy but also to millions of patients in the United States and other parts of the world, its progress and innovative capacity have now been damaged. Your doctors will confirm that the great advances of medicine and surgery of the past thirty or forty years could not have been possible without parallel great advances in drugs. There are, for example, many surgical operations which cannot be carried out without the aid of wonderful new drugs.

What has happened in the last few years? The rate of innovation in the American drug industry has fallen disastrously. The cost of innovation has multiplied many times. The cost of testing a new drug to satisfy the requirements of the modern FDA is extremely high and often prohibitive. So it is that the American drug industry is falling behind that of other parts of the world, notably Western Europe (except to the extent that European drug companies are subsidiaries of American companies, which increasingly do their research in Europe rather than America).

As a result, millions of Americans have had suffering imposed upon them and a sizable number have died precisely because the discovery of new drugs is no longer possible at the rate that it formerly was. That's regulation for you. What is perhaps worse is the utterly inflexible rule of the Delaney Amendment which Congress was foolish enough to adopt, when it was decided that all that was necessary to ban any drug was evidence that any animal had acquired cancer as a result of ingestion of that drug, however unlimited in quantity. This is typically the kind of inflexibility which removes the virtue of regulation even where in principle there might be some.

Then Mr. Morrison told us about the wonderfully beneficent work that OSHA could do, if only it did not play politics. Now the idea behind OSHA is not new. You have had safety laws and regulations for many years. They started in England, naturally, because industry first started there; and in all industrial countries there have been safety and health regulations for a long time. They can perhaps always be improved, and there is nothing wrong in principle with the desire or intent to improve them, though wise men know that there are limits to improvement in practice. Whether improvement should be a federal or a state matter is a separate question. If there were time I would energetically argue that this is par excellence a state, not a federal, matter, but I need not do so here.

Notice, however, what happens when a modern regulatory body makes an attempt at improvement. It falls victim to the well-known disease of bureaucracy, and must do so. For a bureaucrat the first law is to keep on doing what you are doing, whether it is necessary or not. The second law is to do more of what you are doing, whether it is necessary or not. The third law is to do something else in addition to what you are doing, whether it is necessary or not. The fourth law is that whatever you are doing, you must do it inflexibly. This malady of bureaucracy is natural. A man does not make a career in a bureaucracy by doing less, that is to say, by working his organization down or reducing the importance of his office or agency. Of course not. He expands the importance of whatever he is doing; and by doing it inflexibly, he cannot be held to account if something goes wrong, for he will be able to show that he followed the rules.

The human race has had thousands of years of experience of bureaucrats. The Roman empire, the Babylonian empire, the long history of the organization of the Catholic church, the France of Louis XIV and of Colbert, his extremely able economic minister, all of them have displayed these common characteristics, this common malady. There have never been, as far as I know, any horses without four legs; there have never been any established or entrenched bureaucracies without these characteristics. Thus it is that even where in principle it may be desirable to improve some kind of regulation, the attempt to do it by bureaucratic control will produce great harm, which of course applies to the case of OSHA.

All this is true even without the playing at politics which Mr. Morrison has adduced as the cause of OSHA's failure or indifferent success. But what else could you expect than the intrusion of politics into the regulatory system? Suppose that the aims of every regulatory body were as perfect as the human mind could make them, and suppose further that every bureaucrat was incorruptible; yet, since the ultimate power of policy decision rests with the people or their representatives and since the people and their representatives comprehend a wide range of disparate groups and interests, how can you have any kind of regulation which is free from politics? It is simply not possible. That is why the wise man, especially the wise economist or political philosopher, looks with an extremely skeptical eye upon regulation. He knows that even in those few cases where in principle it may be defensible, he should eschew it unless a most powerful case is presented for it, so powerful that it overrides all these characteristics of bureaucracy and of the political milieu in which it must work. So much for OSHA.

Now let us look at some of your other regulatory bodies. Mr. Morrison mentioned one or two, but we need to consider more of them. Take the granddaddy of them all, the Interstate Commerce Commission, founded in 1887, almost a century ago. This was the first great experiment in interstate regulation of what was then one of the greatest industries, the railroads. To cut an extremely long and shabby history short, there is no doubt the railroad industry of the United States has been crippled, in some parts almost destroyed, by the ICC. Yet most railroad men have long regarded the ICC as their friend and protector.

Of course it is always possible to suggest that when an industry goes under, some extraneous factor is at work that would have been there anyway. The rise of the automobile, the truck, and the airplane would of course have presented the railroads with difficult problems, and would certainly have eroded much of their business. But the virtue of policy always demonstrates itself best in those cases where an industry is fighting difficulties. The vice of regulation by the ICC has demonstrated itself over and over again in that it has reinforced, not abated, the influences which were digging the railroads' grave. By establishing a compulsory cartel the ICC forced arteriosclerosis upon the managements of the railroads. The ICC's controls produced a type of railroad manager who is very distinct from the quick, adaptable, and energetic businessman of the authentic American tradition, and whose major concern is to wine and dine with the ICC and to placate its bureaucrats. At the same time, by recognizing cost as the essential basis for rates, the ICC produced a hothouse milieu for featherbedding unions. Thus it is that the railroad industry has declined well below the level to which it might have been forced in a free market by the competition of the automobile, truck and airplane.

The CAB is essentially similar to the ICC. It has not yet had time to ruin the airline industry. In any case it so happens that the thrust of the airline industry in recent years has been upward in more senses than one. It is alive and perhaps well, though its return on capital is not satisfactory for a growing industry. But if the CAB were to have as long a turn as the ICC has had, the world might some day write an obituary notice on the once-great American airline industry and compare it with the airline industries of perhaps more fortunate, because less-bureaucratized, countries. I admit that I cannot say that there are such countries at present.

I have already talked about the FDA. Now consider the Federal Communications Commission. It has delayed and distorted the technical development of the broadcasting industry, which otherwise would have given you a greater choice of programs through cable television and other devices than you have with your three national networks. The FCC is a typically bureaucratic organization.

What about the CPSC (the Consumer Products Safety Commission) which is a Johnny-come-lately among regulators? Consider only one of its interests, the automobile, obviously a vitally important matter since every American wants one and may want two or three. The idea that this is an example of private affluence in the midst of public squalor, as has been alleged, is nonsense and indeed nonsense on stilts.

What has happened to the automobile? To date the cost to you of all the mandatory safety devices that have to be built into the automobile outside of California now amounts to about $750 per vehicle, and in California the figure is higher. That is a great deal of money per unit. Consider the millions of people in America whom you call the poor. Of course what Americans call poverty is wealth in many other parts of the world. In America even the very poor require or desire a car, but they may not be able to afford a new car. They buy a secondhand, thirdhand, or fourthhand car. The loading of extra forms of equipment for safety purposes means that on the average the usage of a car will lengthen because the initial cost will be higher. That means that there will be relatively more second, third, and fourthhand cars; and that means that there will be less safety because cars get less safe as they grow older, on the average. In addition you make millions of people poorer than they need otherwise be.

You may say, and I imagine that Mr. Morrison would be in accord with this, that cost does not matter in this case. What does the cost, say $750, matter, against one life saved? I confess that I do not know how to measure one precisely against another, but courts of law have been doing it for years in negligence suits. The fact is that cost does matter. If it were not so, you could save many more lives by abolishing the automobile, while suffering the enormous consequent cost.

Here we come to a fifth law of bureaucracy. In bureaucratic action costs do not matter or are subsidiary, except where they are costs to the government or to the regulatory body itself. Then they matter exceedingly. The CPSC, the FDA, and the rest, establish guidelines on the basis of physics, chemistry, biology, and the like. They do not ask themselves whether the benefits of their decisions are worth the cost to the people, because it is not their business to do so. That question the people have to ask themselves.

To tell the truth, no regulatory body could answer that question even if it wished to do so, because it cannot be answered successfully except by the separate judgments of the millions of people in the economy, for some of whom the decisions may be worth the cost while for others they may not. Some people, for example, will deliberately pay more for, say, a Volvo, if they believe what the Volvo people say, namely, that it beats other cars in safety and durability. Others will deliberately choose to pay less for a car with less safety built into it. As the Cockney says, "Yer pyes yer money and yer tykes yer choice."

That is precisely the merit of a free market, a free economy, and a free society. Because you are allowed to pay your money and take your choice, you are able to tailor your resources to your needs optimally, except in those few minimal cases where the goods or services required, which alone may properly be called "public goods" in the economist's terminology, cannot be effectively obtained by individual choice.

A similar picture is presented by the FPC. Some may consider it incredible that anyone would think of deregulating power and light companies. Well, Professor Stigler of the University of Chicago has demonstrated that as far as rates are concerned it does not matter whether such companies are regulated or not. That may not prove that regulation is positively bad, but equally it must also mean that it is unlikely to be good. Of course there is a great deal more to utility regulation than this, but one rarely meets a champion of regulation who understands the many diseconomies which arise in the typical state regulation of power, light, gas, and telephone companies.

Consider the National Highway Transport Safety Administration. The NHTSA lays down numerous rules for road safety. Thus at its behest the Department of Transportation not long ago required stronger air brakes in trucks and buses. What happened? There were more accidents. That was because the way the NHTSA worked was a way of producing the opposite of what was needed.

The most important, the most fundamental, thing to be understood is the nature of a market. Mr. Morrison expounded it in a way that millions of people habitually do. Yet he and they misunderstand it. A market arises satisfactorially when there are two factors at work; on the one hand the governmental factor and on the other hand the freedom of each person to act according to the signals produced by the economic activities of other persons. Both are necessary. But almost everybody who attacks the idea of a free market assumes that it comprehends only the second and fails to recognize the importance of the role of the first. The market is a case of the interaction of those who write and administer the rules, and those who play the game. It is not a case of anarchy, in which the players do what they like because there are no rules. Nor is it a game in which the rule makers do the playing.

Suppose that in baseball the umpires from time to time, or in particular situations, told the batters where to hit, how to hit, and which balls to hit; instructed the runners to steal this or that base; ordered the pitcher to throw now a fast ball, now a curve ball, and now a slider; what kind of game would you have? It is not enough to say that you would have a poor game. There is more to it than that. Your players would become progressively incompetent. You would not develop fine batters, pitchers, or fielders. To make it worse, the umpires themselves would be quite incompetent to give the best instructions to the players. So they would have inflexible rules. Every third ball would have to be a curve ball, every fifth a fast ball, and so on.

This is precisely what is happening in most of the Western world, especially in Britain and to a large and growing extent in the United States. Once you have the growth, perhaps the all-pervasive influence, of governmental regulation, then the businessman himself (that is, the player) gets less and less expert. He is less and less on the ball, if I may use that metaphor, and then he gets blamed more and more for delivering less successfully. Thus the real cause of his degeneration is not perceived. On the contrary, the less smart, agile, adaptable, and skilled he becomes, the greater then appears to be the need to take him over or regulate him more. Taking him over is likely to be even worse than regulating him. Then the umpire does not merely give instructions to the players; he picks up the bat or ball and tries to be a player himself. Of course this is a large part of the explanation of the decay of the British economy.

What produces fine players is the freedom for them to make their own playing decisions, subject to a well-devised and well-administered framework of law. But it is not only the players who degenerate under the impress or intervention of regulation; the regulators themselves become less and less competent. Why is that? Because just as the players are at their best when free to act at their discretion within the rules, as American businessmen once were and perhaps still are, so too the rule makers and administrators are at their best when they confine themselves to the making and administration of the rules.

You will not find any example in ancient or modern history where a government has been efficient, humane, liberal, and civilized, while attempting to do more than making and administering the rules. True, there are very few cases where they have limited themselves properly and intelligently to the making and administration of the rules. That is why the history of human government is one predominantly of evil and perversity. But one of those few cases, in many respects the most brilliant in human history, was the case of the Founding Fathers of the American republic and the way they and their successors understood and applied the American Constitution for almost the first century and a half of its life. What has happened to it in the past forty years or thereabouts has changed it fundamentally, has changed it for the worse, and has so changed it because of the people's failure so far to see what kind of big economic regulation and associated economic policies have been sinking them into.

Morrison

It is wonderful to hear so many things that were conclusively shown, conclusively demonstrated, and established beyond a doubt. It is a wonder we have not changed already with all this conclusivity. For instance, we were led to a unitary theory of the decline of the British Empire, having everything to do with regulation, having nothing to do with World War II, or the loss of raw materials, or a hundred other causes. We were told that the ICC is entirely the cause of the demise of the railroads. The facts that the railroads had a monopoly in 1887 and that since that time we have cars, trucks, airplanes, and a lot of other innovations do not have very much to do with the railroads' decline.

We have also heard that the FDA has no business deciding whether a drug is effective. You, the consumer, should decide this yourself. Let us suppose that you are in the doctor's office, you are terribly sick, and you do not know what is wrong with you. The doctor has five thousand different pills, pushed on him by drug manufacturers, and the FDA does not give any clue as to whether they are safe. What are you supposed to do, have your own little laboratory? Is the doctor supposed to have his laboratory, or is there anybody we can rely on? The answer, it seems to me, is that you, the consumer, cannot make your own judgments in a situation like that. It does not make sense to make such a judgment. It does not make any sense because it will not work.

We hear a great cry about the lack of innovation. The reason we are not innovating is that there simply are not that many chemicals that are worth experimenting with. We have had the major breakthroughs. Those days are over. The drugs are all pretty much what they were before, and people are simply fussing around with new combinations to accomplish the same thing. I happen to have a rather healthy skepticism toward the efficacy of a lot of these drugs. I do not think that they help very much, and I am very pleased that somebody besides me and my doctor, who is already overworked, is doing something about it. No doubt a few people have been made to suffer because of the absence of these drugs. But no one has demonstrated that the long-term costs in fact do not exceed the short-term benefits for most people.

Mr. Shenfield's laws of bureaucracy are all very clear and very direct, except that one of them happens not to apply to the CAB. It is the chairman of the CAB and his staff, among others, who are advocating the deregulation of the airlines. Therefore, Mr. Shenfield's theory that leads all bureaucracies downhill does not seem to apply in every case.

But just as there are laws of bureaucracy, there are laws of business. One of the laws of business is that every businessman is out to make a buck. I think that is a good law, but one we ought to take into account when we are deciding whether the businessman should do the testing of drugs. And incidentally, to correct the record on that point, it is the manufacturer that does the testing of drugs, not the FDA. The FDA simply evaluates the test results given to it by the manufacturer. When we realize that the manufacturer has a rather strong bias about which way those tests come out, both as to efficacy and safety, it is not too much to view those test results with a little bit of healthy skepticism. And then what? We say, "Well, the bureaucracy won't work so we should let everybody do it by themselves, and unless we are absolutely convinced that the bureaucracy is going to be perfect, we should not do anything." That does not seem to me to be much of an answer. It does not seem to me to be much of an answer to occupational safety or safe drugs. And to decry the fact that the bureaucracy does not function perfectly does not mean that it should not exist at all.

I suppose that my skepticism about letting people take harmless drugs is in part based on my skepticism about whether a lot of these drugs are in fact harmless to begin with. If I could be assured that there were only about half a dozen drugs on the market, and if I could be sure that each of the individuals in the United States who took those drugs had read the scientific and promotional literature, and if I could be assured that they had sat down and evaluated the literature and were competent to do so, I would be a little less troubled by the chance that they are wasting their money.

But I am afraid that it is very easy to con people into believing that something will be effective, to give testimonials not based on scientific data but on simply the willingness of people to say that they were cured.

I suppose that if I thought that the marketplace were indeed perfect, I might be willing to allow society to have those added costs of frivolity imposed upon it. However, because I doubt that the marketplace is anywhere nearly that effective, I think that the balance comes down in favor of limiting drugs that in many cases are not going to prove to be harmless in use.

It is not quite true that a person is not forced to take saccharin. Fortunately, or unfortunately—depending on your point of view—saccharin is not labeled on all the products that contain it. If you buy a little package that says saccharin, you know that you are taking it. But you may not know what else it is in, and in that sense your free choice is limited. I agree that free choice is worth something. The question is, How much? How do you evaluate free choice? I think it is important and that you just have to look around, but free choice is not the answer to everything. Obviously, if you had free choice across the board, many would think that people should, for instance, be able to buy heroin on the open market because it is their free choice to kill themselves; it is their free choice to do what they want to with their lives. Are there no constraints on free choice? I think our society is not prepared to say that. If we are not prepared to say that, let us not answer these questions by simple free choice vs. no free choice, but let us look at the policies involved in each determination.

Let's assume that all the people who sell bread in the San Diego area got together and agreed upon the price. If you are a consumer, if you want to buy bread, it is going to cost you the price that those people agreed upon just as much as it would cost you the same price if some government agency set that price. And you are no freer to buy that bread below that price if everybody got together and did that, than you would be if the government set the price.

If the lawyers say that you have to have a lawyer in a transaction, or that lawyers may not advertise, that is as much as a gun pointed at the heads of the lawyers, as it is at the people who are affected by the nonadvertising, of not knowing what the price is, of interfering with the free market system, as it would be if it was the government. This is so because the lawyers are able to disbar an attorney who violates the rules. It is no different from government regulation if you get beneath the surface of who is doing the regulating and ask whether they have the power to enforce the rules. And if the power to enforce the rule on bread is determined because you can not get the bread from any-place else because all the people who are selling it in San Diego are agreeing to a certain price, that is as much of a control as it would be if the government did it.

There are very few people I know who think that the government is perfect and that the government does not make mistakes. The fact that government makes mistakes only means that we need people to keep an eye on what it is doing. I find it interesting that Mr. Shenfield favors antipornography laws—that he does not believe that such laws are regulatory.* Who are we hurting by having people reading pornography in the quiet of their own homes? I am not denying that somebody has to protect children, but do we not protect children? It is rather interesting that we get a nonregulator calling regulation part of the law. I do not understand how we decide what is not regulation. Why should people not be free to decide what they want for themselves? Are we not grown up enough to do that? I do not understand where the dividing line is between regulation and nonregulation.

Now, what about the $750 cost per car? Of course, that figure ignores the medical savings, the medical expenses that are incurred every time somebody's head goes through the windshield. It ignores the fact that there are lots of other people besides the person who bought the car who may be subject to economic hardship, not to mention physical and mental suffering. When people buy cars, they do not think about those kinds of consequences; they think about the chrome and the fins and the flashy color. And somebody has got to look out for people when they are not looking out for themselves.

Shenfield

Mr. Morrison's statement that somebody has to look out for certain people is absolutely typical of the regulator. The people do not think, so he has to think for them. Is it true that you do not think when you buy a car? You know nothing about the performance, the acceleration, even the safety. Is that true?

Even if the statement were true for 90 percent of the people, it still would not be a solid reason for regulation. Why? Because if one of the automobile manufacturers lost 10 percent of his main market, he would go broke. And if there are 10 percent of automobile buyers who are skilled and intelligent, who read the trade journals, who are perhaps maybe engineers and mathematicians

*See the summary that follows of Professor Shenfield's rebuttal and comments in which he discusses pornography laws.—Ed.

who know about performance, the producer has to cater to them, and in catering to them he caters to the 90 percent of dummies (if there really are 90 percent of dummies).

American free enterprise, so long as it has been allowed to be free, offers the American consumer marvelous choice, and the consumer has wonderful experience in exercising that choice. If you tell any supermarket manager that the American homemaker does not know how to shop rationally, he will tell you that she is the most careful, thorough going decision maker he knows of. And that is why he has to engage her attention in all kinds of what some people would call tricky, underhanded ways. The fact is, of course, that they are not underhanded. They are ways of countering, to some extent, the marvelous skill of the American consumer.

But in any case, when the American consumer buys something that is bad, the market gives him an immediate chance to change his mind. He can sell what he has; he can buy another thing next week. If it is a short-term commodity such as soap or detergent, his wife can buy a different product next week. If it is a durable commodity, like a house or a car, he can take a loss, of course, but he can sell it. But when you buy a regulator, when you buy a politician who is the presumed master of the regulator (though in practice he is not) you can't change him for two, four, or six years. And when you buy him, you have got to take all the points that he is selling you. You can not choose among them. In the free market you can buy a red tie and a blue suit, but in politics, no sir. If you buy a red tie, you have got to buy a red suit, and if you buy a blue tie, you have got to buy a blue suit. That is the fundamental difference between the market and the process of regulation.

In the case of the FDA, I was talking about effectiveness, not about safety. The point is that with all the millions of different kinds of human beings and human metabolisms and human makeups, who would know better how to choose a drug for effectiveness—not safety—than all the many doctors there are? These doctors know their patients better than do people in the FDA, which says: Bingo, this is effective, this isn't. I leave the rest to your common sense.

If you take drugs, when you cannot personally check the drug for safety, and as Mr. Morrison said, the doctor does not have a private lab, there is a case for the FDA to test safety. Also when it comes to toys, and you have children playing with them, once again there is a case. But when it comes to the automobile, you are dealing with an adult purchaser; the basic rule must be that only if you can show something really dangerous that the adult purchaser could not possibly think of, such as that it was falsely alleged to be safe at any speed, should you have a regulatory body come in.

In matters of safety, I see the very strong possibility that it is a proper function of government up to a certain point. It is not easy to say what that point is, but I concede that. Safety is a different thing from effectiveness, price, quality, and so forth. Moreover, lawyers in the English-speaking world have always understood that the laws of contract and tort would be different in the case of children than in the case of adults. Thus, for centuries in the English system, a minor has not been bound by certain contracts, even though he has the benefit of those contracts. It is proper, because a minor is a case of diminished responsibility. The concept of diminished responsibility and therefore of extra protection for children has been in English law and American law for hundreds and hundreds of years.

This is not a case of regulation at all. It would be all right, I judge, to have stricter rules when it comes, for example, to children and pornography than when it comes to adults and pornography, though I do not know exactly what those rules should be.

However, I am in favor of antipornography laws. I know that it is extremely difficult to decide exactly which pornography shall be allowed, where the line is drawn. I know all those difficulties, but I am in favor of these laws. But I do not call them regulation. They are part of the legal framework in which people must be free to print and speak what they like, especially under the First Amendment. But the First Amendment itself is subject to a legal framework. You will remember what Mr. Justice Holmes once said, about nobody being free under the First Amendment to falsely shout "fire" in a crowded theater? Therefore I am in favor of such laws, but I do not regard them as being of the regulatory kind that I have talked about.

To have a law dealing with pornography you do not need any regulatory body, you do not need any bureaucrats except maybe the police, and the district attorney of course, but the police and the district attorney are part of the administration and the enforcement of that framework of law I talked about. The defects that I mentioned as being built-in, bureaucratic defects, do not apply here unless you call the district attorney or the policeman a bureaucrat, of course.

The difference is this: Long before anybody even heard of the word regulation, we in the Western civilized world had laws about pornography. I readily concede that I could easily be hoist on my own petard in any particular case of pornography. I do not know; nobody knows the answers to exactly where you draw lines, but that is a separate problem.

Mr. Morrison admitted that government makes mistakes and we said that doctors make mistakes. Consumers make mistakes; everyone makes mistakes. However, Mr. Morrison did not seem to consider the fact that government mistakes are inherently different. Someone who uses saccharin might be making a mistake. That person might get cancer, but no one makes you take saccharin; no one gives you cancer. Every single decision the government makes is forced on us, at the point of a gun, because that gun is always there. If you disobey the law, eventually they come and get you.

It would be easy to present a long list of false, even fraudulent, advertising by the minions of government. However, the real point is that human beings are human beings, and whether in business or in government, some will engage in dubious and undesirable practices. The question is, "What are the constraints?" And in private business, given a well-devised framework of laws of contract, of tort, and of corporations, the constraints of the market have been proven by two hundred years (many more years, in fact) of success, whereas in the case of the politician and the bureaucrat, the constraints are extremely defective.

Throw the rascals out. No people in the world should have learned that lesson better than the Americans. Think how many times Americans have "thrown the rascals out" only to get new rascals. And the point is, that it did not matter much, when the rascals' power was strictly limited in a nation that understood the meaning of a government of laws, not of men. The constraints in the political field, where you cannot change what you have bought for two, four or six years are far less effective than the constraints in the field of the market.

The case of bread does not wash in two ways. In the first place, if all the bakers of San Diego agreed to charge 50¢ a loaf, and no less, how long do you think that agreement would last if there were no government sanction behind it? One of the bakers would soon discover that he could greatly increase his revenue by selling at 49¢. All these private cartels, if they had no government agency behind them (like the CAB and the ICC) would not last.

In the second place, part of the framework of law is the prohibition of such cartels. Now in the case of the "regulation" or control of the legal profession, of course such control has the sanction of the law and that is really why it proceeds. If, for example, a private citizen, untrained as a lawyer, went to the court and complained that his fundamental rights of freedom of activity were infringed because he was not allowed to give legal advice and appear in a court, the court would throw him out. That is because under the existing law, the court agrees that the lawyers should have this particular "regulatory" function. Now whether that is a good thing is another matter. But, without the sanction of the law this cannot happen. It does not work. It is a big question whether such regulation is a good thing in the case of professional services, as distinct from the sale of bread, or soap, or something else.

Russia and all the other Communist countries give you a perfect illustration of what happens when you take regulation to the nth degree. Very often, a champion of something will say, "It is unfair to take it to the nth degree." But that is a good test of the nature of it, especially when in fact it is moving to the nth degree. The importance of agriculture is of course wonderfully illustrated by that case. There was a day when Russia, or rather the Ukraine, was the breadbasket of Europe. Britain in the nineteenth century imported immense amounts of grain from the Ukraine. That was completely killed by the Communists, and millions of Russians have indeed died of starvation, as they did under Stalin.

Take the case of California. California agriculture is a miracle of productivity, intelligence, and enterprise. But narrow-minded people often say, "Ah, but California is wonderfully blessed." It is the same old mistake, just as you might say that the United States is blessed from coast to coast with marvelous resources. There were people who lived in California, a few of them, a thousand years ago; simply living in California did not make anything of them. The better test is this: Compare California with other parts of the world, notably Europe, that are just as well blessed. There are plenty of parts of Europe that have a climate as good as California's, soil as good as the Central Valley, the San Joachin Valley. But the efficiency of European agriculture does not compare with the efficiency of California's agriculture. That is because, essentially, the spirit of free enterprise, free experimentation, freedom to judge what you want to do, was less in Europe than it was in California.

Many of the people who developed California agriculture have been in this country only two or three generations at most. Take Italians, for example; many of them came from Piedmont and Lombardy, and developed agriculture here. They did not develop agriculture as successfully in Italy. But do not imagine that the Po Valley does not have large space and plenty of good land; it has. But it does not compare in productivity with California. The spirit of freedom and enterprise has made this country, and you are closing the windows on it.

What I said about my own country was terribly and frighteningly true, but it had nothing to do with the abandonment of the Empire. Notice I do not say loss, because we never lost it, except in the case of 1776 and 1783. But aside from that, we never lost it; we abandoned it, we gave it away. But it had nothing to do with the decay of the British economy, and indeed of the British polity. Switzerland has never had an empire. Modern Germany does not have an empire. Japan does not now have an empire. But they are successful; they are prosperous because they have by and large (not wholly; but by and large) espoused the free market method for dealing with scarcity and the problems of the economy. Britain could have done the same, without the Empire. And what has happened to our society therefore has nothing to do with that side of British fortunes. It has had to do with our economic and social policies, and they are essentially the same as those that have gripped the minds of the American people in the last generation or more.

I want to emphasize in dealing with the elucidation of the maximum freedom of choice, or the optimum freedom of choice, that one must be very careful in using the word "harm." Harm is a very harmful word; it has several meanings. Some kinds of harm are actually harmless, or even beneficial. For example, if I build a better mousetrap and I put my competitors out of business, some say I harmed them. But, of course, I have benefited everybody; I have benefited society because, in the competition with the other mousetrap makers, I have done a better job. But some will call it harm. So be very, very careful. It is the commonest thing for somebody to complain of harm, when all that has happened is that he has failed in due and right and proper competition.

I think it is impossible to give a definition, a limit for maximum freedom of choice, that will stand up completely to analysis and apply to every kind of case. That is why there are lawyers. That is why there are legal philosophers. They have been wrangling about things like this for centuries, and they will continue to do so. But I will say in language that both a lawyer and an ordinary citizen will understand: we must have freedom of choice up to the point at which there is a clear and present social danger, perceived to be such by the majority of the people at the time.

Americans know what is meant by the rule of clear and present danger. If in fact you could guarantee that all pornography were seen only in the closet by adults and only by freely choosing adults, you might say it is entirely unnecessary to have any laws about it. But we cannot guarantee that. We have the problem of public pornography from which you cannot defend children.

It goes even further than that. I hold with Edmund Burke that a good society is free, but it is a disciplined society also. As Burke said, "their passions forge their fetters." Here he was talking about people who do not have self-discipline. It is right, I would say, that a civilized society should have certain minimum standards of conduct that mark public behavior.

No free society has ever proceeded on the basis of free choice or no free choice. A free society proceeds on the basis of maximum free choice against minimum free choice. Maximum, of course, is not 100 percent free choice; it is the maximum possible choice. That is how America became rich and free. After all, Americans are no different (at least 80 percent of them) from their European ancestors. Why are they richer than their European ancestors? Why are they freer, still, than their European ancestors? Why? The answer is not that they came to a country with marvelous resources. Those resources were there a thousand years ago. The Indians did not make anything of them. The Americans made of them freedom and wealth to a higher level, a greater degree than their ancestors had in Europe, which also is endowed with marvelously rich resources. Americans accomplished this precisely because the level of freedom in this country for approximately the first century and a half was deliberately raised in comparison with what it had been in Europe. It was raised not to 100 percent, because that is impossible, but as high as it could be in a civilized society. Maximum free choice, then, is the rule for a good society.

5

Land Use Regulation at State and Federal Levels

Richard D. Lamm and
Bernard H. Siegan

Richard D. Lamm

When one talks about local versus state control over planning, one is not talking about an "either/or" subject. I do not deny that both planning and decision making should take place at the local level.

I find, however, that if we leave land use planning and decision making all to the local level, it does not serve the public interest. It is important that we not ignore the overwhelming evidence of recent public policy decisions in favor of giving states a larger role in decision making. I would like to quote from *The Quiet Revolution in Land Use Control*, published by the Council on Environmental Quality.

> The real problem is the structure of zoning itself, with its emphasis on very local control of land use by a dizzying multiplicity of local jurisdictions. While the Standard Act was a *state* enabling act, it was nonetheless an *enabling* act, directed at delegating land use control to the local level, historically at the city level where the problems which called zoning into being first arose. It has become increasingly apparent that the local zoning ordinance, virtually the sole means of land use control in the United States for over half a century, has proved woefully inadequate to combat a host of problems of statewide significance, social problems as well as problems involving environmental pollution and destruction of vital ecological systems, which threaten our very existence.

> It is this realization that local zoning is inadequate to cope with problems that are statewide or regionwide in scope that has fueled the quiet revolution in land use control. A recognition of the inadequacies of local zoning must not, however, cause the values of citizen participation and local control, which local zoning so strongly emphasizes, to be submerged completely in some anonymous state bureaucracy. Although the governmental entities created by the states to deal with land use problems are statewide or regional rather than local in orientation, these innovations have never involved a total usurpation of local control, and have rarely constituted an attack on the integrity of the local zoning process. . . .

> The innovations wrought by the "quiet revolution" are not, by and large, the results of battles between local governments and states from

which the states eventually emerge victorious. Rather, the innovations in most cases have resulted from a growing awareness on the part of both local communities and statewide interests that states, not local governments, are the only existing political entities capable of devising innovative techniques and governmental structures to solve problems such as pollution, destruction of fragile natural resources, the shortage of decent housing, and many other problems which are now widely recognized as simply beyond the capacity of local governments acting alone.[1]

Ultimately, the problem of local land use decision-making is that it is a perversion of the "Adam Smith effect." Let me explain that. Adam Smith believed that every man, in seeking his own self-interest, serves the greater public good. The "invisible hand" and other forces would operate to maximize the general welfare. As our grandfathers discovered, Adam Smith's faith was not capable of solving the economic problems of the postindustrial world.

The same discovery applies to land use issues. Proponents of local planning and decision-making continue to believe that the sum of the actions of the fourteen thousand separate land use decision makers in the United States amounts to some kind of comprehensive overall plan. In fact, it does not. There has to be some state overview of the major impact decisions, simply because all of these local decision makers operating from their local perspectives do not guarantee a livable framework that we will want to leave to our children.

A U.S. Senate report described the situation as a feudal system under which the entire pattern of land use development has been controlled by thousands of individual local governments, each seeking to maximize its tax base and minimize its social problems.

Replacing this chaos of self-interest are new laws, taking a wide variety of forms but all sharing a common theme: the need to provide some degree of state or regional participation in the major land use decisions that affect our increasingly limited supply of land.

That is the clear trend of state legislation, whether it is a regional body like the San Francisco Bay Conservation and Development Commission, or a statewide authority like the Hawaiian system. In Vermont, in Wisconsin, in Maine, in the regional district of the Twin Cities, there is a recognition that taking only a local perspective creates long-range problems.

This in no way negates the fact that 90 percent of the land use decisions must continue to be made at the local level, be it where a stoplight should be located in San Diego or what the building patterns should be in Beverly Hills. But in certain limited and highly important areas the state must play a role.

The prestigious American Law Institute has been struggling with a model land development code for a number of years and their studies have uncovered numerous situations where lack of an overall state plan has actually discouraged economic development. Thus the major source of opposition to the proposed Everglades airport was the fear that local governments would encourage the development of commercial and industrial facilities in that area around the airport.

Land use planning has often been criticized as being contrary to economic growth and development. In fact, it can be a positive factor in clearing the way for orderly development.

New Jersey learned this the hard way. The failure of local governments to agree upon a plan for the development of the Hackensack Meadows stymied the development of this important area for many years. So, whether the issue is fair housing or filling in a bay, the idea we are really talking about now is perspective. Perspective to ensure that local governments do not allow their own constituent spheres to outweigh completely the interest of a broader section of society that is entitled to greater concern.

The federal government has also recognized the need for regional review of local government decisions. The process requires that there be a regional review of applications for federal assistance under the terms of the many federal grant and review programs in the state.

The Department of Housing and Urban Development has done similar things.

What kind of issues need this larger perspective? Issues that require a degree of sophistication beyond the means of local authorities. Very few of our counties in Colorado, for example, have the sophistication to pass on whether a nuclear plant should be placed in a given community.

A second category would be issues involving questions of great magnitude, such as the location of a transmountain diversion project.

A third category deals with decisions that will have great impact on populations across some imaginary jurisdictional line, downriver or upwind of some large project.

States ought to try to delineate their jurisdiction over certain categories of decision making, and they should keep this power very limited, but there is a responsibility on the part of the state to make sure that other people, beyond the local constituency, have a chance to make their opinions heard.

It is ironic, having stressed this point of view, that my own state, Colorado, does not have an effective statewide body for making high-impact decisions.

The Colorado legislature tends not to practice what I preach: anybody who lives in Colorado would confirm that in a minute. We've made a few inroads, although certainly not on the scale of Vermont, Florida, or other states.

I recognize that when you allocate new powers at the state level you are entering a much larger controversy—the question of what level of decision making is performed at what level of government. We in Colorado are very jealous of our powers vis-à-vis the federal government, so I am sympathetic with the feelings of local officials about their concern for preserving their autonomy.

Just the other day one of our congressmen called up and asked our school officials about the number of calories in the Colorado school lunch program, apparently because the federal government is considering setting some kind of national standards. I felt like saying, "Great, you've got the CIA under control, you've got foreign policy all solved, now you've got nothing better to do than to tell us how many calories we should serve in the state school lunch program!"

In many cases, the federal government has overreached and gotten involved in decisions that should be none of its business. But this doesn't necessarily argue against greater state involvement in land use decisions. One of the reasons for more federal control in local issues is because of the failure of the states, their abdication of their responsibility to deal with issues on a state level.

The mayor of Denver goes to Washington thirty times for every time he makes a two hundred-yard journey across the mall to see the state government. There's a reason for that—he knows where the action is; he knows where the people who can solve his problems are located. The fact that people go to the federal government for help is partially due to the inability of the states to solve many of their pressing social and economic problems.

Land use is one of those problems. Land use decision making should be lodged at the level of government most suited to deal with the problem. Usually, that will be the local level.

But there are definite cases where there are large impact decisions, where there is jurisdictional overspill, where a state role is needed.

Often local governments are too small to afford the professional talent needed to do a good job in planning. There is little incentive for them to pursue other than the local parochial goals. State governments can take a more complete view of the problem, balancing the needs of one subregion for jobs with the needs of another subregion for recreation and open space. It can back up its plans with a formidable dollar investment, with state highways and state-funded schools. It can coordinate land use with social and economic policies. In many states these decisions are made in the public eye, as opposed to the often private and occasionally questionable planning decisions made at the local level.

The state's intervention then, should be limited to the minimum needed to protect the nonlocal interests. There are two aspects of this involvement. The first is mandating local land use planning and regulation, passing the necessary enabling legislation to insure a thorough analysis at the local level. The second role is to review certain of those local land use decisions that, because of their magnitude or their sophistication, demand state scrutiny.

Bernard H. Siegan

My position is that there should be less regulation of land use at both the state and federal levels of government. The existing problems of land use can best be solved by deregulation, not increased regulation.

Let me begin by referring briefly to the experience of zoning in this country, so that we can better understand the operation of land use controls. We have a rich history of zoning regulation, even just considering the part of which the public is aware. Areawide land use controls arrived in 1916 in the form of the New York zoning resolution, the country's first zoning ordinance. It was a modest ordinance containing three use districts: residential, commercial, and unrestricted; five classes of height districts; and three classes of area districts. At my last count, New York had sixty-six zoning districts and a host of other controls never conceived of by the framers of its original ordinance. A similar story applies to other cities. Small, modest ordinances in time develop into very complex and complicated ones. One reason for this is, of course, the change in conditions, techniques, and thinking that occurs over the years and is reflected in our laws. But there are two other explanations for the uncontrolled growth of zoning.

The first is that zoning has been the story of unrealized expectations. We have now had four or five different zoning systems or strategies in this country. Each has been introduced with what has turned out to be greatly inflated rhetoric as to what it would accomplish. And each in turn has for the most part, failed to meet the expectations created by that rhetoric. The result, every time, is a new effort at the drawing boards, producing more and severer rules and regulations which, experience suggests, are not likely to be more successful than the previous ones.

The current situation in San Diego provides an example. The existing zoning system has been deemed inadequate and a great many promises are being made as to what the new proposed five-tier zoning policy will accomplish. One gets the impression that even if only some of these promises materialize, this city will surely be another Valhalla.

Another reason for the proliferation in zoning regulations is that the process is basically one of resolving differences between various special interest groups in the community. No matter how perfect the zoning plan, some people will be helped and others hurt by it. Immediately after passage of the ordinance, the losers, experience shows, start doing those things that will make them winners. Owners of property will seek to rezone it, to increase its value. Homeowners and conservationists will lobby to downzone property and civic groups will move to overcome the inadequacies they discover. The courts may also effect significant changes. It will not take long before the original plan has been reduced to not much more than a historical document, having innumerable amendments grafted upon it.

The dominant factors in zoning have been public pressures and political influences—the factors to which officeholders respond. Matters such as efficient use of the land, conservation, consumer demand, and sound planning have been subordinate and often nonexistent considerations unless they coincide with popular pressures.

The question arises, can these widely recognized problems be solved by state or federal land use regulations? The simple answer is that political pressures, moral and legal corruption, and bad laws are not confined to local government. A second answer comes from the experience of regulation in this country. That record has been an extremely poor one. The most immediate example is the regulation of the airlines. President Carter, Senator Kennedy, Ralph Nader, and Milton Friedman, all agree upon substantial economic deregulation of the airline industry.

The evidence is rather clear that airline regulation has been harmful to the nation. A study by the General Accounting Office has concluded that a reduction in federal regulation of airlines during a six-year period would have resulted in fare reductions ranging from 22 to 52 percent. The lower fares would have resulted in savings to domestic air passengers on the order of $1.4 billion to $1.8 billion per year. The Carter administration has now also proposed deregulation of rail and truck rates by the Interstate Commerce Commission, thereby joining Ralph Nader and Milton Friedman who have long championed this view.

Even in the area of health and safety, it is most questionable how effective regulation has been. Consider the case of the Food and Drug Administration, and I do not refer to the current flap about saccharin. Some very extensive studies have shown that while the FDA is keeping bad drugs out of the market, it may be excluding or delaying the introduction of an even greater number of beneficial ones, such as those which might help relieve or control heart disease and cancer.

Numerous studies have been made of the regulatory agencies and many of them have been printed in the *Journal of Law and Economics*, published by the University of Chicago Law School. The editor, Professor Ronald Coase, has this to say about these studies:

> The main lesson to be drawn from these studies is clear; they all tend to suggest that the regulation is either ineffective or when it has a noticeable impact, that on balance the effect is bad, so that consumers obtain a worse product or a higher priced product or both, as a result of the legislation. Indeed, this result is found so uniformly as to create a puzzle; one would expect to find in all these studies at least some government programs that do more good than harm.[2]

Accordingly, based upon the history of zoning and other regulation, the lesson should be clear that additional regulation of land use should not be imposed unless there is extremely strong cause for it and even then, only if it is very likely to accomplish its purpose.

Using these criteria existing proposals for state and federal land use controls fail. To demonstrate this, let me discuss with you the objectives of the principal groups seeking such regulation. These include the environmentalists, egalitarian-civil rights groups and a portion of the development industry.

The environmentalists seek to carefully screen or prevent development in areas considered environmentally sensitive. What are environmentally sensitive lands? The definition is not as simple as it may appear. This was evident in the bill sponsored by Congressman Morris Udall and others, which would have partially subsidized state land use programs, and which nearly passed the U.S. House in 1974. That bill's definition of areas of environmental concern was so broad many of us thought it included most of the land west of the Mississippi River. In a subsequent bill introduced by Udall and others in 1975 (H.R. 3510), the definition was refined and among other things, eliminated agricultural land, but it still included vast territory. Thus, one paragraph of the section defining lands designated as areas of critical state concern includes "natural or historic lands with significant scientific, educational, recreational or aesthetic values, such as significant shorelands or rivers, lakes and streams, rare or valuable eco-systems and geological formations, significant wildlife habitats and fragile areas." This language could cover enormous areas.

Regardless of the language or intent of its sponsors, it is not likely that all development will or can be prohibited within these areas. In all probability, what will happen is much more of what is already occurring under local zoning. There would be less development, more land would be used for urban purposes, and real estate prices and rents would tend to increase. However, relatively few of the critical areas would be preserved in their natural setting.

There are two basic reasons for this. First, there are the "taking" and due process provisions of federal and state constitutions which limit the extent to which private property can be regulated. Second, the regulatory process tends to solve controversies through some compromise formula, an approach which would be reinforced in this situation by the constitutional provisions I have mentioned.

The history of California's coastline regulation, established in 1972 by public initiative, discloses how land use controls would probably operate in areas of critical environmental concern. In 1973, over 6,200 permit applications were received by the six regional commissions given permit power under this law. Of these, about 5,200 or 83 percent, were granted. In 1974, of the approximately 4,700 permit applications received, some 4,400, or 94 percent, were approved. Such figures do not accurately reflect the regulation's impact, however. To obtain a better understanding of what these numbers mean, consider Professor Bruce Johnson's analysis of the operation of the Santa Barbara Coastal Commission, on which he served. During the first fourteen months in the life of that commission, it approved 95 percent of the applications received for single-family dwellings, but allowed only 60 percent of the single-family units requested on these applications. While 77 percent of the multifamily applications received approval, only 51 percent of the units applied for were accepted.[3]

Accordingly, we may conclude that if a developer applies for a permit to build 100 units on his five-acre tract adjoining the Pacific Ocean, he will, after considerable delay, red tape, maneuvering, and possibly a nervous breakdown, have his request whittled down to say, around 70 units. That's what is referred to in regulation as "balancing."

The five acres in our example will still remain in private ownership and will not normally be accessible to the public, except possibly for an easement to the coastline that would be required, but would have more theoretical than practical value. It is questionable that better views would be provided since the buildings might also have to be aesthetically compromised. The question that now presents itself is what happens to the thirty units that were disallowed? One probable answer is that these, along with other disallowed units, represent unsatisfied demand and would in time, cause greater or more rapid development of the coast, something entirely inconsistent with the aims of the initiative. It is of course possible that the thirty units would never be built, in which case society will have lost the benefits of approximately three quarters of a million dollars worth of construction benefiting business, employment, tax revenues, and housing supply and there will be less housing at higher cost.

Possibly these thirty units may find their way into existing vacant land within a developed city. But they would then reduce the amount of land available there for other projects. Another alternative is that the disallowed units will increase demand for building in rural, undeveloped areas at the expense of other environmentally sensitive land, or of land used or suitable for agriculture, grazing, and mining. The result in this case would be more spread and sprawl, exactly those horrors from which regulation is supposed to protect us. But this consequence is not an unusual one these days. Slow- and controlled-growth policies have caused development to leapfrog the areas so restricted and sprawl and spread farther and farther into areas that are or should be used for other purposes such as farming, grazing, and mining.

An article in the *Texas Monthly* describes the situation very succinctly. It concludes the following about the growth policies of the Austin (Texas) City Council:

> The irony is that the most anti-growth council in Austin history may have done more to bring about urban sprawl than did any of the pro-developer councils that preceded it. Over 75 percent of the homes built in the Austin metropolitan area last year were outside the city's extraterritorial jurisdiction.[4]

The relation of these experiences to the proposed statewide controls should be apparent. A similar pattern is likely to occur with respect to areas of critical environmental concern in demand for development, and much more than just the California coastline would be involved. Development would take place, but with less intensity of use, and while there would be more open space, it would be privately owned and not normally accessible to the public. The proposed state controls would accomplish more of what the proponents say they want to prevent: instead of conserving a precious resource, more of it will be misused and wasted.

Developers have not been blind to the regulatory dynamics. In October 1975, an article in the *San Diego BCA Builder* advised its readers on how to cope with public proceedings:

> It is generally advisable to be prepared to give something up. Don't go into the public hearing with a bare minimum proposal. Be ready to barter something away.[5]

Many developers can be expected to try to beat the game by asking for more than they really want; that would mean that frequently the entire process would accomplish little more than waste the public's time and money, increase development costs, and further undermine the credibility of government.

Some civil rights groups are also demanding state land use controls. They want the state to require all or most municipalities to allow development of projects catering to minorities and low- and moderate-income families. They condemn exclusionary zoning and argue that it can only be overcome by state or federal laws. One problem with their approach is that zoning or land use regulation will not build housing and the housing they are talking about requires government subsidies which are not very plentiful these days. Nor are they likely to succeed in obtaining the kind of land use regulations they want. Most legislatures are suburban-rural dominated, or strongly beholden to such forces, and they are not about to force low- and moderate-income housing down the throats of unwilling municipalities. The State of New York provides an example. Its Urban Development Corporation had for many years the power to override local zoning ordinances and develop low-income housing in suburbia. When it finally attempted to implement this by announcing a number of projects, it was stripped of that power by the New York legislature in 1973. There is one state, however, that has made an effort to deal with this problem, but its results are minimal and possibly counterproductive.

In 1969 Massachusetts passed an antisnob-zoning law under which developers of low-income projects could appeal local denials to a state agency. In the first five years under this statute, comprehensive building permits for less than 3,000 units were issued, which constitutes even less than tokenism, considering there are some 350 cities and towns in the state with a population of just under six million. Despite the encouragement of this law, developers have found it too difficult to obtain the subsidies and finances to build the housing and fight City Hall.

It might be said that even this number is better than nothing. Such a conclusion is highly questionable. Cities and towns that contain or have zoned for small amounts of low-income housing have self-righteously claimed fulfillment of their obligation to mankind. They say they should now be left alone to do as they wish with the rest of their zoning. Some courts have accepted this line. Thus the Federal Appeals Court upholding the severe growth restrictions of Petaluma, California, justified its decision, in part, on the basis of the small amount of zoning for lower-income people provided in the city's plan.[6] The court noted that the city had allowed for about fifty units of such housing annually. The justices were seemingly unperturbed by the fact that the development controls validated probably excluded ten to fifteen times that number of conventional units. This is a very poor tradeoff for the housing consumer, poor and rich alike, especially considering how little funding is available for subsidized housing. But the idea has politically attractive features which could be implemented in state-controlled zoning to create an even more exclusionary result.

Some developers favor state and federal controls over zoning in the hope that the higher levels of government will provide better for them than the localities have. These enterpreneurs believe that state controls will bring about a kind of one-stop service so they would have to go only to one state agency for a development permit, instead of being continually bogged down by an array of public bodies at the local level. All the evidence suggests that this is no more than a pipe dream, although it was very seriously advanced by supporters of the Udall bill. State land use control will bring with it requirements that a plethora of state agencies pass upon various aspects of development proposals much as now occurs at the local level. The problem for most developers would be compounded, not relieved.

The proponents of higher-level land use regulations are doing what seems to come instinctively these days—ask for more or a different kind of government regulation when the existing ones have failed. This attitude represents what Dr. Samuel Johnson called, when speaking of another endeavor, "a triumph of hope over experience."

Not only would state or federal land use regulations not solve the many problems seen by its proponents, it would be harmful to our society. Consider how it would affect the development industry. At the present time the complexity of local regulations has forced many small builders to drop out. They do not have the funds to hire lawyers and experts that are so necessary these days for those who have to cope with zoning. The troubles of this group would be intensified when a new set of regulators emerges at the state or federal capitols. The bigger and wealthier builders are in a much better position to hire the needed help. As a result, we might in time lose the very great efficiency, creativity, and imagination of the small builder, and that indeed would be a serious loss for the country.

Faced by criticism of this sort, both Udall bills for national land use policy contained provisions safeguarding property rights. These provisions stated that nothing in the act "shall be construed to enhance or diminish the rights of owners of property as provided by the Constitution of the U.S. and constitution and laws of the state in which the property is located." For the Rockefellers and Gettys, this kind of rhetoric may be comforting; but for a small landowner it is close to meaningless. No matter how wicked, reprehensible, and confiscatory a regulation is, a bolt from heaven will not strike it dead. It can only be declared unconstitutional or illegal by a court of law, and this means that the owner must be in a position to use costly and lengthy court processes to sue for such a ruling. From the moment the regulation is even contemplated—perhaps just a glimmer in a planner's eye—those financially able will begin employing lawyers and experts to protect their interests.

The big owners and developers have the capabilities and will often modify or defeat regulations. While the state authorities may find it difficult to overcome wealth, they will encounter far less opposition from those owners who cannot fight back. The latter group may have to settle for lower prices, await future appreciation, or just pray that someday the meek will inherit the earth. In other words, state and federal controls will operate to do exactly the reverse of what is written and intended in the Udall bill. The regulatory process will, in effect, enhance property rights for the wealthier owners and diminish those of the less-affluent owners.

Finally, let us consider the impact of additional state and federal land use regulation upon the country. In spite of the dangers of refueling inflation, the national government is spending billions upon billions of dollars to reduce unemployment, stimulate, the economy, and increase housing starts. Housing in particular has been badly hit during the last three years with starts substantially decreased. At the national level, the emphasis is clearly on greater economic growth and any reduction in gross national product such as came to light with the recently revised figures for the last quarter of 1976 seems to send shivers through Congress and the administration. A contrary perspective prevails at many local government levels. There, through the use of zoning laws, efforts have been under way to manage, slow, or even stop, growth. The impact of the billions being spent nationally to promote growth are being countered by local efforts to restrain it.

These policies at the local level are not only harmful to the economy, but they hurt the most primary of environmental concerns: employment, better housing, and better housing conditions. The people desperately in need of a better quality of life are those who are unemployed and living in substandard housing. Under our system, only private industry can help alleviate these troubles, but its efforts are currently being hampered by the innumerable restrictions and regulations of local government. New regulations at higher levels will only add to the problem. The proposed state or federal regulations will cause a large number of new rules to be superimposed on a large number of existing rules and at the very least, that will result in confusion and uncertainty for owners and land developers. Two or three government levels will then have a piece of the zoning pie. It may be necessary to hire experts in the locality, in the state capitol, and possibly, if national land use is enacted, in Washington as well, just to determine what the new rules are.

The situation demands deregulation. We should start dismantling the regulatory processes which harm the economy and prevent people from acquiring the best and most desirable shelter. There surely should be no greater regulation of land use at either the state or federal level.

Lamm

One of the problems in deciding a public policy issue is analyzing an argument for what it is and, conversely, for what it is not. Let's take some of these things in order and talk, for instance, about the regulatory system.

I think that I would be foolish to attempt to justify the entire regulatory system, and I am not going to do it. I think that we have actually, in many instances, overregulated and not had the appropriate regulation. However, I know few people who think that the total answer to this problem is to deregulate all those things that we have historically regulated, and I find, and I hope you find, that there would be some mischief in this.

In Colorado we have come up with a partial, not a perfect, solution because in these areas there is never a perfect solution. But at my request the legislature passed the nation's first sunset bill. Under this bill we look at every one of our regulatory apparatuses, and we say, "Is it performing the functions that it should be performing? How can it be streamlined? How can we make it more effective? How do we make it more cost-effective?" We are starting that review right now and are rather interested, by the way, to see the people's reactions. In some instances we will abolish a regulatory apparatus. I am not sure that we need the landscape architects in our state regulated just so that they can tell the sod carrier that the green side is up! But I very much believe that in most, or at least many, of the instances where we have had regulation, it is important to streamline that regulation, not to deregulate. You can mention on the one hand saccharin; on the other hand we had thalidomide. I think that the Colorado answer is much better.

It is true that in many instances the special interests have sought regulation themselves, to keep out of the wind and rain of competition. But I think this is no reason to turn 180° and suddenly go in another direction. I find that course to be a mistake. Reforming is better.

With regard to additional layers of land use, I find that again it is a reform of the system that we need, not simply additional layers. We want to make the system more effective. I think it is tempting but simplistic to say, in terms of Houston, the example that is often given in this area, that we should return to a simpler time when we did not have any regulation. Every time I get a parking ticket I feel that government interferes too much in my business. But I think, to be realistic, that we need a certain amount of regulation. How can you run a modern-day city without parking tickets? Are you really not going to regulate public utilities, trucklines, all the other things that are regulated?

Government has a very important role to play in terms of the cost of developmental growth. It is interesting to see how many times the builders talk about governmental controls, but they are the first ones to ask government to insert itself into the process because they want a utility line extended to their subdivision, or they want telephone lines, or they want the trash service out there, or they want roads. So in land use planning, as HUD [the Department of Housing and Urban Development] has shown very simply in its publication, "The Cost of Sprawl," in terms of a good bargain for the citizens, good well-planned growth by competent people, intelligent land use decisions can save the taxpayers a lot of money.

With regard to regulation benefiting larger companies, I would like to say a couple of things. First, about the federal system. It is valid to worry about the feds because of their historic expansionism. Regulation does benefit larger companies. However, I think that important areas can be controlled through streamlining the regulation. The federal government, as has been said, has long had a national growth policy under the modest name of the Federal Highway Act.

That would be my second point. Whether we like it or not, the government is in this business, so we should not really look at these areas simply; we have to look at land use beyond its regulatory, control type of focus to a positive program of regional development and public investment. We make decisions every day, lots of decisions about how we invest the public's money. I think that in terms of a well-developed land use program, looking at it not simply as a method to stop things, but as an intelligent way to develop an area, we end by making a very good investment for the taxpayer. The existence of many communities causes a fractionalization of governmental authority, but there is a great deal to be said in its favor. We do want home rule; we want a certain amount of rule. The rule, however, should not go beyond the needs of the community. That can be handled in two ways; by the state saying "when it goes beyond you have to stop," or by simply removing those powers of municipalities that will impact other municipalities, impact the region, and impact the state.

I think that one of the fastest-growing units of government has been local government. And in fact, we probably have more local government than we need in a lot of instances. Part of what we are showing in the sunset process and other things is that we can streamline government and actually have no more employees and no more money spent but a lot better job being done. In this area, in making sure that you have some sort of state-level regulatory apparatus, you are going to end up saving taxpayers money by limiting the counties' capabilities in this respect. It is better to centralize. Regulation can be inflationary; it can be disconcerting to deal with; it can be corrupt; it can be all of those things. The answer, however, is to reform it, not to abolish it.

Places in Colorado (and there are a number of them) that don't have any zoning laws are analogous in some respects to Houston (although I do not want to push that too far). I think that the costs of not having land use devices, not having the developer pay for some schools, having to provide some roads—these costs are coming back in a very big way to haunt the people. It is a time bomb that ticks, and every year it ticks louder. What would this country be like without Euclidian zoning? It might not be perfect the way it is, but I think that overall, as imperfect as the system is, land use patterns—making people put in sewer systems, making them pay for some of the costs of their development—has been indispensable in providing a certain livable community in most places.

Euclidian zoning arose as an idea of a control point to make sure that we do not have an industry or a pig yard in the same place where we have neighborhoods; and it has been a thou-shalt-not type of thing. Do we go back? Do we retreat into our last fifty or sixty years of history, or do we go forward and say that a land use plan can very easily, and should, be made into a positive growth plan for the area. You simply take critical areas, wetlands, prime agricultural land, and you make a decision that in fact those are worth saving, and then you have a very positive growth plan about where industry is going to be in the future, where highways, public investment, colleges and universities are going to be. And consequently, I would not like to retreat from zoning but to go forward, not in a control apparatus but as a way of making a positive development plan for an area.

Siegan

Let me just give you an idea of the kind of problem that comes with regulation. One could say, "Let's just solve those problems." But let's look at a specific situation for the kind of complexities involved. The governor and others have said that 90 percent of land use decisions apply to the local level, that they have no impact beyond the local level. I sometimes look at that figure, and I think that a typographical error has been made. It is often the reverse because if you look at almost any land use decision that a small community makes, you see that it concerns people outside that community. When a small community has a housing development, people from outside the community come to occupy that housing. Most of the land use decisions within a community relate to housing. Gas stations and shopping centers also cater to a great many persons who do not reside in the locality. Accordingly, the major impact of regulation in suburban and rural areas is on people outside the community, and these areas have grown more than the large cities in recent years. Using the idea of letting the state do those things that apply to the state and letting the locality do those things that apply to the locality sounds simple, but in practice such a course may create enormous problems, and even an enormous amount of litigation. It also perils home rule.

I propose a rule for all regulation: Before we impose regulation, we should have a very, very clear reason for it, and we should also be sure that that regulation will accomplish its purpose. If we use that test, I would not be disturbed about regulation. However, I cannot conceive of that situation in this particular context. What I am suggesting is that the state get out of the business, as far as it can, of regulating local land use decisions and start encouraging municipalities to do away with those enormously complex, difficult regulations that, I think we all agree, are creating a great many problems.

Governor Lamm and I both started by discussing the problems of local zoning. There are two ways to go; one is to get more regulation, the eternal solution to the zoning problem. If the local zoning does not work, the state will have to do it. If the state does not do it, the federal government will have to do it. I do not know who is next because there really is a stopping place somewhere. The point is that the history has been so difficult, so adverse; the same kind of factors apply basically at the state level that apply at the local level. We should look at this in a mature way and say, "This is an area where regulation simply does not work. Let's start rolling those regulations back."

Now, I do not mean to suggest that the same kind of outcome results with every other conceivable kind of regulation, but I do emphasize that it certainly applies generally to the use of land. There are, of course, some minimum regulations that are clearly necessary to control land use and do meet the kind of criteria I suggested. However, the experience of Houston illustrates that not many regulations are needed. That city's system has operated for a considerable period of time, not only successfully, but also with minimum commotion and corruption, and without the disturbances that we here in San Diego see and that we see nationally.

Consider the matter of aesthetics, a subject that I find very difficult to discuss because aesthetics is a very personal kind of thing. Nevertheless I might mention this. Builders around the country go down to Houston to see two- and three-story apartment developments. The reason is the enormous variety and the enormous competition that occur there. That is a point that I really want to emphasize—the competition that is not permitted in areas that have a great deal of regulation. The competition in Houston has resulted in enormous gains— aesthetically, for rents, for costs. Moreover, there are covenants in Houston to safeguard against the possibility of glue factories or slaughterhouses being built in residential areas.

The regulation of expression illustrates what should be done in the case of land use. We have constitutional protection of expression and we allow regulation of expression when there is a compelling state interest. That kind of standard can be used for economic as well as speech regulation. Under that standard there must be a very, very good reason before regulation will be upheld. We are doing something in expression that should give us an idea of what we can do with respect to other regulation. Expression is unlimited up to a point at which a "compelling state interest" justifies control. And that kind of criterion, I think, is applicable to zoning; it is applicable to a lot of regulation that we have.

There are serious problems to be faced, whichever level of government regulates land use. I have found in my practice of law that one of the most frustrating things is standing before people who have enormous power—for example, zoning boards—and talking to them, realizing that they understand little of what I say. Developers spend thousands and thousands of dollars to bring all kinds of experts and exhibits before a zoning board, and the board is simply not capable of fully comprehending what is being presented to them. That is what happens when you have lay boards that operate in the zoning field.

However, people will tell you that the great benefit of local government is accessibility, the fact that you can go to the town meeting, or you can go see your city clerk and tell him what is wrong or right. They lose these benefits when controls are placed at higher levels of government. My standard is to get rid of as much control as you can at all levels because, as far as I'm concerned, whether local, state, or federal government tells me "you may not do this," the import is the same. It is not the entity of government that bothers me; it is what happens to the freedom of the individual. And if that freedom is curtailed at the federal level or at the state level or at the local level, something should be done about it.

By regulating and by restricting, we are going to hand unborn generations a very bad society; we are going to hand those generations a society that may be lacking in freedom. We may be handing down a society that has slums, that has unemployment, that has lack of competition, and that has the other undesirable consequences that regulation causes.

The standard I have suggested for imposing regulation would protect both existing and unborn generations. Society would not be limiting freedom, except when it is essential to do so. A democratic society should have standards for regulation that all can understand and abide by. We do it now on a hit-or-miss basis, on political pressure, on individual influence. That is very bad. We have achieved the goal I am talking about in expression, in religion, in many civil rights. We should not regulate; we should not encumber individual initiative unless there is a very, very good reason to do so.

Notes

1. Fred Bosselman and David Callies, *The Quiet Revolution in Land Use Control* (Washington: Council on Environmental Quality, 1971), pp. 2-3.

2. Ronald Coase, "Economists and Public Policy," in *Large Corporations in a Changing Society*, ed. Fred J. Weston (New York, N.Y.: New York University Press, 1975), p. 169.

3. M. Bruce Johnson, "Piracy on the California Coast," *Reason*, July 1974, p. 18.

4. Paul Burka, "Liberal Education," *Texas Monthly*, March 1977, p. 109.

5. Harrison Waite, "How to Preserve an Endangered Species," *San Diego BCA Builder*, October 1975, p. 10.

6. *Construction Industry Association* v. *City of Petaluma*, 522 F.2nd 897 (9th Cir. 1975).

6

National Health Insurance: The Kennedy-Corman Bill

Lester Breslow and
Harry Schwartz

Lester Breslow

The Kennedy-Corman bill establishes a federally financed and administered health insurance program for the entire population covering a comprehensive range of services with no cost sharing by the patients. This measure is designed to bring good medical care equitably and at a reasonable cost to all the people in our country. The first question is whether medical care is really desirable for people's health. That's not as simple a question as it seems. Mr. Schwartz and I would agree that medical care is overrated as an influence on health. Social conditions of life, physical environment, personal habits, seem to have a much greater impact on health than the doctor or any other part of what we call the health care system.

Still, medical care is important for health: to prevent measles and polio; to cure many cases of appendicitis, brain tumors, streptococcus infections; to alleviate diabetes and many forms of heart disease; to find cases of breast cancer among women over fifty years of age, and cervix cancer at any age or high blood pressure among men when the likelihood of death can be vastly reduced. Yes, medical care really can sometimes save one's life or substantially reduce disability. Furthermore, its power is increasing. For example, with amniocentesis, a high-risk pregnant woman can find out whether or not her pregnancy is likely to result in a child with Down's syndrome, a common form of mental retardation. And then she will have, through medical care, an opportunity to decide how to proceed. Probably we can all agree that good medical care can be extremely valuable to our health.

Do the people in our country have such medical care? Some do, some don't. I do, and I presume that most of the people here do. We seek it for our families, we'd like it for all our countrymen. But they do not all have good care—some because they don't seek it, a few because they live in remote parts of the country where it is impractical to maintain high-quality care close at hand. But tens of millions of Americans do not have adequate medical care because they cannot afford it under the present system. As a nation, we have made various efforts to deal with that problem; thus far we've failed. Public hospitals and clinics for the poor have sunk to lower and lower—in some cases, scandalously low—levels of physical condition and professional service.

Medicaid offers different benefits in various states—generally poorer levels of care in poorer states because of state options as to how much will be spent. In 1971 New York and California took nearly 40 percent of the federal outlays for Medicaid. The poor states get the crumbs. Low-income, marginal workers generally have very inadequate health insurance plans compared to the kind maintained by and for most of us who are more affluent. When unemployed, millions must resort to using public programs. The federal government starts and stops immunization programs for measles, polio, and other conditions, leaving children so unprotected that, for example, in San Francisco in 1975 there was an epidemic of measles, with several hundred cases reported (and probably several times that number unreported). This number was greater than that reported in any of the preceding six years, and the disease is one that we've been able to prevent since 1963. And a comparable epidemic is just getting under way in Los Angeles.

Now suppose people, whether poor, middle-class or well-to-do, do get to the available medical care. Far too much of it is not up to an adequate standard of quality. Many physicians still perform procedures for which they are not qualified. Study after study shows unnecessary surgery, often by persons who are not trained as surgeons even though we have, according to data assembled by very respectable surgical organizations, more than enough well-trained surgeons for the country.

It is not only surgery where this problem of quality exists. Dr. Jack Meyers, the current president of the American College of Physicians in the December 1976 *Bulletin* of that organization, said, "As a general internist, I continue to be appalled about the wide-spread over-use of diagnostic procedures, particularly on hospitalized patients on medical services. Such over-use is a major factor in running up the cost of medical care." It should also be pointed out that it is not only a matter of cost but also of hazard when one is subjected to certain diagnostic as well as therapeutic procedures.

Grossly inadequate is too nice a term to describe the present American medical care situation, certainly compared to what it could be with our resources and the typical American organizational ability and diligence. And what are we paying for this grossly inadequate care? Over 8 percent of the gross national product. The typical American works one month of each year just to support grossly inadequate medical care, and the cost is going up. While the nation has been experiencing substantial inflation in the economy as a whole, the inflation in hospital, physician, and other medical care costs has been much greater. Are we getting our money's worth? That's the question which above all others is forcing consideration of national health insurance.

Among the several proposals, the Kennedy-Corman bill is the only one that would deal squarely with the major problems our nation faces in health care— inequity, highly variable quality, waste, and spiraling costs. The bill would make everyone in the country eligible for services just because he lives here. There would not be one program for the poor, another for the unemployed, another for the elderly, as proposed in other bills. Everyone would be eligible for precisely the same benefits. It would go a long way toward ensuring decency, humaneness and equality in health care. The program would pay for nearly the entire range of personal health care services: physician's services, hospital services including outpatient services, home health services, optometry, podiatry, devices and appliances and dental care for children up to the age of fifteen at the outset and extending beyond that in succeeding years. All of these would be available with no deductibles and no copayments as are commonly imposed in current insurance practices. With some limitations, there would also be psychiatric services, nursing home care, and drugs.

The legislation would establish a cost and quality control system. Surgery, except for emergencies, would be paid for only if provided by qualified surgeons. And the Board of Administration could extend that kind of control to other speciality services. A quality control commission would develop national standards for health care providers, including required continuing education, and be charged with otherwise developing standards for high-quality care. The bill would bring the present federal programs—Medicare, Medicaid, programs for military dependents—as well as the services now provided by a myriad of private insurance companies, all into a single administration. It would thus eliminate overlapping systems and multiple wasteful procedures.

It would be paid for half by a payroll tax, to which the employer would contribute 3.5 percent of payroll and the wage earner 1 percent of his earnings up to about $21,000; the other half would come from general federal revenues. Expenditures would take this form: a small amount would be set aside for contingency reserves and for the development of additional health care resources. All the rest would be divided among ten regions of the country on the basis of recent patterns of use and expenditure. Funds would be budgeted for each of the regions, each category of service (so much for hospital care, so much for physicians, and so on). Each year a determination would be made of the amount to be spent in each region in each category of services—hospital, medical, dental, drugs, and others. Regional and local planning would be strengthened to set priorities, for example, to curtail unnecessary inpatient services and expand preventive services. Hospitals would operate on an approved budget in advance, not charge whatever they liked for services. The hospital administrator would negotiate and know his budget so that he could concentrate on improving services rather than scratching to collect payments for them day-by-day. Health professionals licensed in the states would be eligible to participate at the start of the program, but would continue to be eligible only if they met national standards and requirements for continuing education, as a quality control measure.

Physicians would have freedom to select their mode of practice. They could choose to be paid fee-for-service within an overall budget collectively controlled by the physicians themselves in each region; or elect a salaried basis within an institution; or enter a group practice prepayment plan like Kaiser; or enter other per capita arrangements. Incidentally, strict quality standards for organized delivery systems such as Kaiser would obviate the kind of scandals we have seen in California with the almost uncontrolled "Prepaid Health Plan" sponsored by the previous state administration.

A couple of questions are sure to be raised: Can we trust the federal government to administer national health insurance? Wouldn't it bungle the job, be wasteful? Let's examine the alternatives. For example, take private health insurance, which has borne a major responsibility for paying for medical care costs over the past several years. You've no doubt seen many accounts of overpayment and failure to deal with fraud by the private insurance companies, resulting in huge sums of money wasted. These have been exposed by U.S. investigators year after year. Walk into a large hospital or a local government agency dealing with claims for payment for health care under our present potpourri arrangement. You will see armies of clerks, hundreds of them in the larger institutions, trying to sort out the myriads of claim forms for the many different private companies and different government plans. Keeping track of who is eligible for what plan, and then keeping track of the varying deductibles and copayments in the dozens of plans is a bureaucratic and very expensive nightmare.

Let me give you one personal example. I was astonished a couple of weeks ago to receive, as a physician, a check from a major private insurance company in California, which I'm sure many of you subscribe to; as a matter of fact, I do myself. It was a payment for a service I did not perform, for a person I did not know. In fact I do not treat individual patients and have never submitted a bill for services. Of course I sent the check back, but I shudder at the cost of straightening out that little bit of nonsense.

Turning to large-scale data rather than anecdotes, in 1973 private health insurance retained $3.3 billion in administrative costs and benefits according to a U.S. Department of Health, Education and Welfare estimate. That was nearly double the $1.7 billion in 1972. I don't know how high it is today, but 1972 and 1973, if you will recall, were supposed to be years of economic stabilization. In Rhode Island during 1975, commercial insurance companies collected $39.8 million in accident and health insurance premiums, approximately $40 million. Of that total, less than $30 million was paid out in benefits; more than one-fourth was retained for administrative costs and profits. That was a good benefit ratio. In the preceding ten years, the average for benefits was less than 70 percent.

Coming back now to governmental operations, the 1975 unit cost of processing a health insurance bill in the division of direct reimbursement in the Social Security Administration was $4.11. That may be compared with the average Blue Cross plans of $4.60 and the commercial insurance company average of $5.64. Thus the fact is that a government agency even now does the job less expensively than do the private insurance companies.

Another point about governmental operation vs. private is that governmental operations are much more accessible to public scrutiny. We can find out more readily what's going on. And bear in mind that whether the cost of processing the bill by the government or the private company is $4, $5 or $6, another comparable, and probably larger, amount must be spent by the hospital in preparing the bills in order to cope with the present jungle of plans, deductibles and copayments.

What will be the total cost of medical care in the country under the Kennedy-Corman program compared to continuing the present situation or adopting one of the alternative plans? Probably no single question in the health insurance debate has generated more downright mischievous, malicious obfuscation than this important question. Some assert that the Kennedy-Corman bill would cost $60 to $100 billion more. That is hokum. The money is already being spent. Practically all of that money would merely be transferred from present private insurance company channels to governmental channels. The employer and the employee—most of us—would simply have the payroll deductions for health care sent by computerized paycheck to the Social Security Administration instead of the insurance company.

During the past eight years, when the federal administration could hardly have been accused of bias in favor of the Kennedy-Corman bill, the government has conducted or commissioned several studies to estimate the costs of various health insurance proposals. Invariably, the range of total difference from the most to the least expensive (including continuing with the present arrangements) is about 10 percent. That's probably within the limit of error in estimation in such large-scale enterprises. The most recent study conducted under the auspices of the Ford administration by consulting actuaries in 1976 gave estimates of total health care costs for 1980 as follows: the present system, $180 billion; American Medical Association plan, $196.6 billion; Kennedy-Corman, $200.2 billion; and American Hospital Association, $200.4 billion. There isn't any substantial total cost difference among the plans. As a matter of fact, the director of the Congressional Budget Office has estimated that the Kennedy-Corman bill would actually save $20 billion annually by 1981 compared with present policy or major alternative plans. And the health care benefits would be clearly much greater.

Now one final consideration in the minds of congressmen must be, what do the people think? A June 1974 Harris poll showed that 54 percent of the American people favored a comprehensive federal health insurance program, like Kennedy-Corman (although it wasn't named), 28 percent opposed, 18 percent not sure. A Cambridge survey in 1975 showed much the same thing. Many church and civic groups as well as labor, other groups, now the National Education Association, have endorsed it. The momentum of popular support is growing.

There is a common misconception of how physicians view national health insurance. A national survey of the medical profession in 1973 showed that 56 percent favored some form—not necessarily Kennedy-Corman—of national health insurance. But those surveyed thought that only 19 percent of their colleagues favored it. It appears that even the physicians are taken in by the AMA propaganda. Furthermore, regardless of how they felt about it, 83 percent of the physicians thought that national health insurance was inevitable, and 62 percent believed in 1973 that it would be here by 1978. Incidentally, the same survey group found that only 38 percent of physicians favored Medicare when it was first passed in 1965, 70 percent favored it a year later, and 92 percent five years later. Such data should give Congress confidence that the country is ready for national health insurance and that people generally want and should have the Kennedy-Corman bill.

Harry Schwartz

In one variant or another the Kennedy-Corman bill has been before Congress and the nation for roughly a decade. It has had powerful support and a large supply of funds and personnel for propaganda supplied by organized labor. Yet it has not become law, and as I write this in mid-1978, (revising my original remarks at the debate early in 1977) it seems less likely than ever that Kennedy-Corman will ever be enacted. Even Senator Kennedy has abandoned some of the principles Dr. Breslow praised in his presentation and has suggested compromises that I suspect Dr. Breslow must find painful.

The reasons for the failure of the Kennedy-Corman approach emerge rather clearly if we analyze Dr. Breslow's case for that bill.

Dr. Breslow has touching faith in magic and miracles. He declared seriously, "The Kennedy-Corman bill is designed to bring good medical care equitably and at a reasonable cost to all the people in our country." Dr. Breslow apparently believes this is possible and all that is needed is for Congress to pass and the president to sign his favorite panacea, the Kennedy-Corman bill.

Over the past fifteen years since President Johnson began orating about the Great Society and the abolition of poverty, the American people have been unhappy participants in a number of efforts to realize similar miracles through the supposed magic of federal government intervention. The best commentary on those efforts is the fact that President Carter, a Democrat, was elected in 1976 by campaigning against the federal bureaucracy, its idiocies and its costs. We have slowly, painfully, and expensively, been taught that the federal government is simply incompetent to accomplish the great social transformations we have asked it to perform.

Government is increasingly seen as the enemy, the extortionist depriving us of the fruits of our labor through exorbitant taxes, the main force producing inflation that robs the old of their savings and their anticipated security, the mad source of innumerable confusing regulations which are increasingly tying American institutions into knots and forcing the expenditure of billions or tens of billions of dollars for low-priority purposes.

The incompetence of government is overwhelmingly evident. Government can no longer assure us that basic precondition of civilized life, personal security of life and property. The school system, run by government virtually from the beginning of our nation, turns out more and more functional illiterates who can neither read, write, nor do elementary arithmetic, even though spending on education mounts endlessly. And if all that were not bad enough we find that governmental incompetence is accompanied by corruption which grows ever greater as the powers of government increase. In the field of health it is necessary only to mention the rampant corruption and thievery produced by the MediCal and Medicare programs.

The central issue between Dr. Breslow and me is that he would expand government still further, give it complete authority and control over our health care in every respect. He looks at the disaster that is American government today and says, let's throw medicine into the pit. After all, he seems to say, why should sick people be treated better than youngsters in school, and why should doctors and nurses have greater freedom than school teachers and principals? Now, Dr. Breslow has spent his career as a bureaucrat, as a well-paid government official. He has never participated in the actual work of treating sick people as it is normally done in the United States by a doctor who does his work and sends his bill. It is not hard to see that behind Dr. Breslow's enthusiasm for Kennedy-Corman is a vision of the huge bureaucratic structure it would create. Is it unreasonable to suspect that Dr. Breslow sees himself as one of the generals of that future army of bureaucratic doctors? His interest in the advancement of bureaucrats is very different from the interests of the American people in getting good, compassionate care when they are sick.

Dr. Breslow has properly and correctly pointed out that there are deficiencies in the existing medical system. Curiously, all the deficiencies he has pointed out are relatively secondary. Not all children are immunized. True enough, but that is true in every country, including nations like Britain which have complete socialized medicine. Some operations and diagnostic procedures are unnecessary. True enough, but one would have to suppose that all doctors are the seventh sons of seventh sons and have infallible foresight to assure that only the absolutely correct number of diagnostic procedures and operations are done.

He also ignores the problem of malpractice—born of suits filed in government courts—which is the basis for much overuse of diagnostic procedures.

In any case, under whatever medical system we have, even Kennedy-Corman if we were so unfortunate as to pass it into law, doctors will make mistakes, some doctors will prove unworthy of their trust and so on. All I am saying is that to point out only the deficiencies of what exists, and to pretend that the nostrum proposed—the Kennedy-Corman bill—will not have similar or even worse problems, is to exercise less than full candor.

We know already from the long and unhappy experience with Medicare and MediCal what is wrong with government medicine of the type Dr. Breslow would make universal through the Kennedy-Corman bill. In a fee-for-service system in which the patient pays, the patient has an incentive to shop around for the best value at the lowest price. He also has an incentive to do without such medical intervention as he judges not worth the price. Under MediCal and Medicare, much of medicine is made to seem free to the recipient. This removes all, or almost all, patient incentive to economize. It is that simple fact which explains why medical costs have skyrocketed since a Democratic president and Congress turned Medicare and Medicaid into law.

The Kennedy-Corman advocates have learned a little from the disasters that preceded them. They would control costs by setting limits and by introducing policemen. Every area of the country would be told it could spend so much for medical care and no more. And meanwhile thousands, tens of thousands, of government policemen would be snooping everywhere to see how the government's money was spent. So what is now advertised as free medical care for all would soon be reduced to making hard choices.

In San Diego should the respirators of twenty-five elderly patients dying of respiratory disease be turned off or should dialysis treatment be denied fifty victims of uremia who require dialysis to remain alive? These are the kinds of hard choices that would be faced. Government bureaucrats, in short, would be given the power to decide which of us will live and which of us will die. The opportunities for legalized murder and for corruption on the grandest scale simply stagger the imagination.

Perhaps our medical system is so bad and so expensive that we have no alternative but to resort to such desperate efforts at national rationing—and make no mistake, that is what Dr. Breslow and Senator Kennedy are advocating—of health care? That idea is simply untenable. It is interesting that Dr. Breslow felt it unnecessary to make any specific, statistical reference to the actual health experience of the American people in his remarks. The reason for his silence is simple. The data do not support his case at all. In recent years, the death rate of the American people has fallen steadily to record lows; the infant mortality rate has plummeted and is now almost 50 percent less than it was as recently as 1965, and the life expenctancy of a newborn American baby is seventy-three years, the highest such figure in our history. Moreover, never before in American history has this nation had so many well-trained physicians, so many well-equipped hospitals, and so much possibility of helping the sick.

I want to conclude by mentioning the chief deficiency of American medicine which Dr. Breslow did not mention: American medicine cannot guarantee us immortality. We will all die—doctors and patients alike—regardless of what medical system we have, even Kennedy-Corman. But while we live, we need a medical system in which we have choices among individual doctors and among different means of organizing medical care. We want expertise, compassion, and, if at all possible, a successful result when we undergo medical care. That is what the overwhelming majority of Americans receive every year in our complex, pluralistic and, yes, expensive medical system. It is that reality, the fact that most patients are satisfied, that explains why Kennedy-Corman has not been enacted into law despite many years of effort by people like Dr. Breslow and despite many tens of millions of dollars spent on propaganda by organized labor and its friends.

Breslow

Unfortunately, a great many Americans are not high enough on the income scale to be able to afford any kind of decent medical care. That is why we do need to ration that 8 percent of the gross national product that we are already spending for medical care to ensure that we do get out of it the greatest good for the greatest number. We have reached, or are closely approaching, the level at which the American people will rightly refuse to pay any more for medical care. The Kennedy-Corman bill would face this situation, and would, as Mr. Schwartz points out, ration medical care. The word "ration" is not so much different from the word "rational." Here we are trying to deal in a socially rational manner with an extremely important issue and trying to get to all our people, as best we can in a democratic society, that which is truly essential for their health care. Of course, if one wishes a pastel phone in his hospital room, he could pay extra for that.

The notion is put forward that the patient determines what medical care he is going to get, that he rations it himself if he has to pay the fee, and that he will not waste it. That is sheer hokum. The doctor rations the medical care. The patient goes to the doctor and pays the doctor if there is no insurance, or if there is insurance, the insurance company pays. After that point, the patient hardly enters into the decision. The decision is made by the physician, and quite properly, with the patient simply approving. But the initiative is all on the part of the doctor, and that is where the expense of medical care arises.

There are millions of people in this country who are receiving welfare assistance as their total, or almost total, income. There are also millions of unemployed and their families, and I submit that by and large those people are not receiving the kind of medical care that we should regard as adequate for America in 1977.

There are various forms of national health insurance, and the surveys that I mentioned were directed toward many forms. One survey asked about comprehensive national health insurance, of which the Kennedy-Corman bill is certainly the prototype, and well understood as such. Other surveys, particularly the ones for physicians, contained no specification about the type. But we are talking about national health insurance—a system of paying for medical care in which the providers of care are sought out by people for their illnesses or for preventive services. We are not talking about some kind of national health service in which the hospitals are owned and operated by the government and physicians are employed and paid by the government. The Kennedy-Corman bill does not establish a system of national health service.

The study of physicians' attitudes was made by John Collin Bliss, a Columbia University School of Public Health professor. He found that only 38 percent of physicians favored Medicare before it passed, 70 percent favored it a year later, and 92 percent favored it five years later. What has always been of interest to me is that organized medicine bitterly opposed Medicare, but they supported Medicaid and were in fact the ones to introduce the Medicaid portion of the law. But now, five or ten years later, as I sense what organized medicine has to say about these two programs, if physicians favor one, it is certainly Medicare. Clearly, there is far greater participation by physicians and hospitals in the Medicare program than there is in Medicaid. I think it is important to read history very carefully.

I want to point out that the inducement under catastrophic insurance would be in exactly the wrong direction for accomplishing what we can with medicine nowadays. It would put the emphasis on the very catastrophic, which usually means, unfortunately, terminal illness. It would put tremendous sums into advancing and using technology at the extremities of life, when I sense that the American people are beginning to turn away from that. They seem to want to die a little more simply, a little more comfortably. Catastrophic-illness insurance would raise the expense of dying, not of living. It would devote medical care dollars to prolonging dying, not living.

Schwartz

I am very pleasantly impressed—I will not say surprised, because I know Dr. Breslow is a very well-informed student of these issues—that he has come to agree with me. The core of the matter is, "Shall we ration medical care as the government wants to see it, according to the government's idea of what is equitable and what you need?" If we pass the Kennedy-Corman bill, the government will decide what you should get. And if you may want more than that, it's just too bad!

There is a school of thought that says if you want to save money, do not bother treating some kinds of brain tumor patients at all. They are going to die anyway. What is the point of giving them an extra six months? If that person happens to be you or someone you love, that extra six months may be extremely important. But if the government is paying for the treatment, it will say that it wants to use the money for something else—not the extra six months for that person who is losing his faculties anyway. We need more money for more swine flu inoculations. That is the kind of decision they are going to be making—and Dr. Breslow suggests that the rationing is related to rationality!

Well, he is about my age, and he and I lived through a system of rationing. I remember when gasoline was being rationed in this country. You know what rationing brings to my mind: black market. And so I can see a system in which the government is trying to ration dialysis treatments to kidney-failure patients, and what this brings in its wake is inevitably corruption. The Soviet Union and the Eastern European countries all have a fine system of socialized medicine, in which all the things Dr. Breslow is talking about are true, including the rationing. Everybody there knows that if you want to get first-class care, you have to pay the doctor or pay the hospital administrator. What the government is going to give you "free" and what you want are two very different things.

For quite a long time, the intellectual establishment of the United States has been very much in favor of socialized medicine. We have been subjected in America to a brainwashing by much of the media that the medical system in America is rotten, no-good, infant mortality is high, and so forth. So they say we need national health insurance. And the interesting thing is that we still do not have national health insurance. The reality of the question is that the pressure for national health insurance—and certainly something as drastic as the virtual socialization of American medicine under Kennedy-Corman—comes from a narrow elite of communicators, union officials, and public health people.

7 The Economics of Free Speech

Milton Friedman

There is a close connection between economics on the one hand and the maintenance of a free society to which the law is dedicated. They are not separate problems. I am going to try to illustrate the relationship between economics and a particular problem in law—the maintenance of free speech, which is in some ways the most fundamental of all the freedoms in our society.

At the extreme, there is a clear and direct relationship between economic arrangements on the one hand and free speech on the other. For example, the restrictions on Alexander Solzhenitsyn's free speech when he was in the Soviet Union were significantly affected by the character of the economic system, and not merely by the particular way in which the Soviet Union chose to use that economic system. Suppose you could stretch your imagination so far as to suppose that a totalitarian centralized system such as the Soviet Union was by some miracle dedicated to trying to preserve free speech. Consider the economic problems that would be involved in doing so. The real test of free speech is the ability of a minority to express its view. Suppose a small group in the Soviet Union wants to propagandize for capitalism. In order to propagandize, it has to rent a hall. Whom can it rent a hall from? All halls are owned by the government. In order to propagandize by putting out leaflets, it has to get a printing press. Where does it get a printing press? They're all owned by the government. It has to buy paper from a government-owned company. It has to have it printed by a government-owned printing shop. It would take an extraordinary degree of dedication to the principle of free speech for each and every one of these people all along the line to be willing to make their facilities available, but even suppose they were willing to do so. Where would the money come from to finance these activities in a society in which the major sources of funds are governmental? There are some wealthy people in Russia, but they are not wealthy in the sense in which they can provide out of their own resources substantial sums of money for campaigns. On the contrary, to finance such activities would require a government fund for the propagation of subversive doctrine. Suppose such a fund existed. It's clear that the demand would exceed the supply—that would be a pretty attractive way to make a living! So with the best of will it would be literally impossible to maintain free speech in a full-fledged collectivist, socialist state.

We seldom recognize the enormous importance of diversified sources of financial and economic support in making it possible for a "nut" to have his say.

You know, today's nut may be tomorrow's prophet. The essence of free speech is to preserve the opportunity for nuts to turn into prophets.

The relation between economic arrangements and free speech is close, long before you get to a full-fledged socialist state. I want to illustrate how close that relationship is in terms of the situation in this country, and in other countries in the West, which we would say are predominantly free societies. Consider, for example, the restrictions that have been imposed in the United States particularly in the course of the past forty or fifty years on various groups in our society. One group in the United States that has been denied free speech in practice, not in principle, is businessmen. Recently I received a letter from an executive vice-president of an oil and gas association. I won't mention names, but I will read what she said:

> As you know, the real issue more so than price per thousand cubic feet [this was with respect to energy legislation] is the continuation of the First Amendment of the Constitution, the guarantee of freedom of speech. With increasing regulation, as big brother looks closer over our shoulder, we grow timid against speaking out for truth and our beliefs against falsehoods and wrongdoings. Fear of IRS audits, bureaucratic strangulation or government harassment is a powerful weapon against freedom of speech.
>
> In the October 31 edition of *U.S. News & World Report*, the Washington Whispers section noted that, "Oil industry officials claim that they have received this ultimatum from Energy Secretary James Schlesinger: 'Support the Administration's proposed tax on crude oil or else face tougher regulation and a possible drive to break up the oil companies.'"

Let me give you another, more subtle example of the restrictions on free speech imposed on businessmen. I am sure all of you, like me, have received from your bank a little piece of paper printed by the U.S. Department of the Treasury which urges you to buy U.S. Savings Bonds. If that piece of paper had been published by a private commercial concern, the Federal Trade Commission might very well castigate it as misleading and inaccurate advertising. I have often said that the U.S. Savings Bond campaign has been one of the greatest bucket-shop operations in history. The government tells people, "You buy these bonds and it will assure your future. This is the way to save and to provide income for your children's education and your retirement." Then it turns around and produces inflation that erodes the value of those bonds so that anybody who has bought a bond during the past fifteen or twenty years has ended up getting back a sum that has less purchasing power, that will buy fewer goods and services, than the amount he originally paid. And, to add insult to injury, he has had to pay taxes on the so-called interest, interest that doesn't even compensate for the inflation produced by the federal government that sells them the bonds and makes those promises.

You may not agree with me. You may think the bonds are a good investment, but I introduced this example for a very different purpose. Do you suppose the bankers who send you this piece of paper believe it? I've asked quite a number of bankers, "Do you think that savings bonds are a good investment for your customers?" They uniformally answer, "No, it's a terrible investment." I say to them, "Why do you send this piece of paper around to your customers? Why are you participating in what I believe is fundamentally a bucket-shop operation?" They all give me the same answer. "The Treasury would be very unhappy if we didn't. There's great pressure from the Treasury."

Not long since, I talked in Salt Lake City with a middle-management executive of a large enterprise who was telling me how terrible he thought the savings bond campaign was. In the next breath he told me how much time he had to spend promoting it among his employees because of pressure from higher-ups who in turn were reflecting pressure from the U.S. Treasury. Do those bankers, or these executives, have effective free speech?

Of course, occasionally there are courageous bankers, courageous businessmen who, despite the cost, express themselves freely. But the public statements of business leaders are almost always bland. They talk in general terms about the evils of government regulation and about the importance of free enterprise, but when it comes down to cases, they are very careful not to be too specific. There are some noble exceptions.

You may say, "That doesn't matter, those are only businessmen; after all, businessmen have enough to do making money, they don't have to worry about free speech." Let's turn to my own field, to academics, and ask, "What has happened to the freedom of speech of academics?" Consider my colleagues at the University of Chicago in the medical school, most of whom are supported in their research by grants from the National Institutes of Health. Which of them wouldn't think three times before he made an impassioned speech against national health insurance? I don't blame them; I'm not criticizing anybody. I'm only trying to discuss the relationship between the economic arrangements we adopt on the one hand and free speech on the other. People ought to bear a cost for free speech. However, the cost ought to be reasonable and not disproportionate. There ought not to be, in the words of a famous Supreme Court decision, "a chilling effect" on freedom of speech. Yet there is little doubt that the extent to which people in the academic world are being financed by government has a chilling effect on their freedom of speech.

What is true for the medical people is equally true for my own colleagues in economics departments who are receiving grants from the National Science Foundation. I happen to think that the National Science Foundation ought not to exist, that it is an inappropriate function of government. Not very many of my colleagues would be willing to endorse that statement in public, certainly not those who have NSF grants. In fact, I've often said that about the only academic who in this day and age has freedom of speech is a tenured professor at a private university who's on the verge of retirement or who has already retired. That's me.

Let's go from the academics and these chilling effects on freedom of speech and look at the relationship between economic arrangements and freedom of the press in a more direct and immediate fashion. You may have heard what happened to the *Times* of London, a great British newspaper, "The Thunderer" as it used to be called. It was prevented from publishing one day by one of its unions. Why did the union close it down? Because the *Times* was scheduled to run an article about the union's attempt to influence what was printed in the paper. That's as clear and straightforward a violation of the freedom of press as you can think of. You may say, "Well, that one didn't involve government." Of course it did! No union can gain so dominant a position without the aid and backing of the government.

Another example from Great Britain is equally pertinent. There is now a National Union of Journalists in Great Britain which is pushing for a closed shop of journalists writing in British papers—and there is a bill pending in Parliament to facilitate this outcome. The union is threatening to boycott papers that employ nonmembers of the National Union of Journalists who are not willing to join and assist their declaration of principles. And all this in Great Britain, the home of our liberties, from whence came the Magna Carta.

To turn more directly to the courts, judges, like intellectuals in general, have shown a kind of schizophrenia regarding different areas of free speech. The courts have tended to draw a sharp line between what they designate as political or cultural speech on the one hand and what they designate as commercial speech on the other. Thanks to the tutoring that Professor Bernard Siegan has given me, I realize that the Supreme Court recently has taken some timid steps toward extending First Amendment rights to commercial speech. It has done so in connection with a Virginia law that would have prevented pharmacists from advertising, an Arizona law that would have prevented attorneys from advertising, and a New Jersey local law that would have prevented people from putting "For Sale" signs on their property. The Supreme Court has declared all these laws unconstitutional. But in each decision, it has been very timid and has continued to insist that there is a sharp line between the two kinds of speech and that the First Amendment gives absolute protection only to political speech, and not to commercial speech.

While I welcome these recent moves, the difference in attitude toward political and commercial speech is still extreme. For example, the owner and publisher of a pornographic magazine, *Hustler*, was found guilty in Ohio of publishing obscenity. Many prestigious intellectuals signed a petition objecting strenuously to what they interpreted as a violation of free speech and an act of censorship. Personally, I do not see much difference between the *Hustler* case, as a restriction of freedom of speech, and the legal prohibition of radio and television advertising of cigarettes. Yet no distinguished, or for that matter undistinguished, intellectuals signed a petition in behalf of the freedom of enterprises to advertise cigarettes—though one, namely myself, did write a *Newsweek* column to that effect. In its decision on the Virginia advertising case, the Supreme Court explicitly said that its decision did not invalidate the government's requirement that advertising bear a warning label such as the one on cigarettes. "The Surgeon General has determined that cigarette smoking is dangerous to your health." Congress has now passed a new law which is going to require all saccharin to bear a similar label. I have yet to see any intellectuals object to that infringement on free speech. Yet suppose a law were passed requiring *Hustler* magazine to carry a warning: "Reading this magazine may be dangerous to the moral health of children, other immature people, and even some mature people." Is there any doubt that such a law would produce an uproar, and that it would be overturned by the first court to hear the case? You cannot maintain that this difference in reaction is because somehow the contents of *Hustler* are more noble or uplifting than the smoking of cigarettes or the use of saccharin. The difference simply reflects what is fundamentally an arbitrary distinction between certain kinds of speech.

To give an even more dramatic example, we have no hesitancy in saying that requiring tobacco companies to put a warning label on cigarettes doesn't infringe on their freedom of speech. There is little doubt that far more human lives have been lost over the past century as a result of Karl Marx's *Das Kapital* than from smoking cigarettes. Would it therefore be appropriate to require every copy of Marx's *Das Kapital* to carry a warning label saying, "Reading this book may be dangerous to your social and personal health?"

Everyone would agree that that's a violation of free speech. Why the one and not the other? Personally, I think it's terrible to smoke cigarettes. I quit twenty years ago and so obviously I want everybody else to quit. Personally, I think Marx's *Das Kapital* is a pernicious and dangerous book. But that does not mean that I believe it is desirable to restrict advertising for either cigarettes or *Das Kapital*. On the contrary, I favor the avoidance of legal restrictions on either the one or the other.

The schizophrenia of intellectuals in general, of courts in particular, extends far beyond regarding commercial speech as somehow very different from political speech. It goes to the whole problem of the supposed distinction between political freedom on the one hand and economic freedom on the other, to the difference in the way that the courts have interpreted the free speech clause and the due process clause. We've seen in the extreme case of Russia, and in less extreme cases as well, that you cannot have political freedom without a very large measure of economic freedom. A large measure of economic freedom is a necessary condition for political freedom—but more to the present point, there is no really sharp line between the two.

Economic and political freedom are not different in kind and it is frequently not easy to distinguish between them. Let me illustrate. Russia does not permit free speech. Everybody agrees that that's a violation of political freedom. Russia does not permit emigration. Is that a violation of economic freedom or of political freedom? Russia does not permit those people it does let go out as emigrants to take more than a few personal possessions with them. Is that a violation of economic freedom or is it a violation of political freedom? Great Britain permits its citizens to emigrate and it permits free speech but it does not permit emigrants to take their property out with them. Is that a violation of economic freedom or of political freedom?

Recently, as it happened, I received another letter that illustrates this relation. This was a letter from Pakistan. It was from an academic at a Pakistan university who had studied at the London School of Economics and who is now back in Pakistan. He wrote, "I have been delving into the political philosophy of liberalism and individualism and have read whatever little on the subject is available in our libraries. . . . It has been my great misfortune that your highly popular work, *Capitalism and Freedom*, is not present in the libraries of this country. . . . Exchange control regulations in this country prevent me from buying it from a publisher in the U.S." Is that a restriction of his economic freedom or of his political freedom or of his intellectual freedom?

Take something closer to home yet. Freedom of choice about where you live is surely more important to most people than free speech as it has been typically defined. Yet the courts have routinely upheld zoning and land use legislation that seriously interfere with freedom. Not to mention the kind of emigration requirements that I was just speaking about, a recent article in the *Los Angeles Times* illustrates the difficulty in drawing the line between economic and political freedom. The story is about a student at a high school in Iowa who is from Nicaragua and is living in this country on a visa to attend high school. Unfortunately for him, he wanted to be self-supporting, so he got a paper route that pays him $9 a week. The Immigration Service found out and it now tells him that he will have to leave the country unless he quits his job. Is that interfering with his economic freedom? Or is that interfering with his human and political and personal freedom?

When a city legislates zoning ordinances that prevent people within that city from making voluntary transactions with people outside the city to buy or sell property, imposing great costs on one or the other or both, is it interfering with economic freedom or human, political freedom?

The line is a difficult one to draw. All of these cases, particularly the housing and the zoning cases, raise third-party effects, neighborhood effects as they are sometimes called. An agreement between two people to buy a piece of land or build a house affects neighbors who look on it. The point I want to emphasize is that those same effects are present in all the free speech cases. There's no distinction on that ground.

Consider, for example, the recent case in which an American Nazi group wanted to have a march in a mostly Jewish suburb of Chicago. That was a clear free speech case, yet there is no doubt that it involved serious third-party effects in the way of a possible riot, imposing costs on residents or bystanders not directly involved, let alone the police costs of enforcing order.

Take such a simple thing as permitting a parade down a main street of a city. That may impose heavy costs on businesses along the way through the loss of custom.

Consider still a different third-party effect. A political candidate campaigns for office by riding around in a truck with a blaring loudspeaker on top. If a commercial truck advertising, let's say, soap or perfume or detergent, were to try to blare out its message on the same streets, at the same volume, there's little doubt that that would be regarded as a serious violation of the freedom of others. But is the message the one is delivering really more important, more reliable, and more trustworthy than the message the other is imparting?

I am myself a liberal in the true original sense of the term, namely, belief in freedom. So I favor both free speech and economic freedom. And I would lean over backward very far indeed with respect to third-party effects in order to preserve both. But that is not my main point in the present context.

My main point is to demonstrate that there is a basic and fundamental inconsistency in the attitude of intellectuals in general, and the judiciary in particular, to the two areas of freedom. I can understand how someone would be willing, in order to protect third parties, to restrict both free speech and economic freedom. That's a consistent position. I obviously can understand how someone would take the position I do—that the social objective of maintaining a free society is so important that a very strong presumption must exist before freedom in either area is restricted to avoid third-party effects. What I cannot understand is the schizophrenic position that almost any cost may be imposed on third parties in order to protect one kind of freedom, namely freedom of speech, but that almost any third-party effect, however trivial, justifies restricting another kind of freedom, namely economic freedom. That seems to me to be a wholly inconsistent position which no reasonably logical, consistent man who understands what is involved can hold.

Index

Index

List of Contributors

Lester Breslow
Dean, School of Public Health, University of California at Los Angeles.

Ronald H. Coase
Clifton R. Musser Professor of Economics, University of Chicago Law School. Editor, *Journal of Law and Economics.*

Milton Friedman
Nobel laureate in economics. Professor of Economics, University of Chicago. Senior Research Fellow, Hoover Institute, Stanford University.

M. Bruce Johnson
Research Professor and Associate Director for Research, Law and Economics Center, University of Miami School of Law.

Nicholas Johnson
Chairman, National Citizens Committee for Broadcasting. Former Commissioner, Federal Communications Commission.

Richard D. Lamm
Governor of Colorado.

Louis B. Lundborg
Retired chairman of the board, Bank of America and BankAmerica Corporation.

Henry G. Manne
Director of Center for Studies in Law and Economics, and Distinguished Professor of Law, University of Miami School of Law.

Alan B. Morrison
Director, Public Citizen Litigation Group.

Harry Schwartz
Member of the *New York Times* editorial board. Distinguished Professor, State University of New York, New Paltz.

Arthur A. Shenfield
Economist and British barrister. Regents Professor at University of California at Davis.

Bernard H. Siegan
Distinguished Professor of Law, University of San Diego School of Law.

Stewart L. Udall
Former Secretary of the Interior.

About the Editor

Bernard H. Siegan is Distinguished Professor of Law, and Director, Law and Economics Studies at the University of San Diego School of Law. He writes a weekly syndicated newspaper column and is the author of *Land Use without Zoning* and *Other People's Property*. He is the editor of *Planning without Prices* and *The Interaction of Economics and the Law*. He is also a contributor to professional journals and other publications, having written articles pertaining to land use, zoning, and urban planning.

Professor Siegan received the J.D. degree from the University of Chicago and was in private practice for many years.